CHRISTIAN MUSIC

IS VOLUME

125

OF THE

Twentieth Century Encyclopedia of Catholicism

UNDER SECTION

XII

CATHOLICISM AND THE ARTS

IT IS ALSO THE

75TH

VOLUME IN ORDER OF PUBLICATION

Edited by **HENRI DANIEL-ROPS** *of the Académie Française*

CHRISTIAN MUSIC

By ALEC ROBERTSON

HAWTHORN BOOKS · PUBLISHERS · New York

First Edition, October, 1961

NIHIL OBSTAT

Joannes M. T. Barton, S.T.D., L.S.S.

   Censor Deputatus

IMPRIMATUR

Georgius L. Craven, Epus Sebastopolis

   Vicarius Generalis

Westmonasterii, die XI AUGUSTI MCMLXI

CONTENTS

INTRODUCTION

The greater part of this book is concerned with music composed for the liturgy of the Roman Catholic Church which, in plainsong and polyphony, has given the Christian world a vast treasure of unsurpassed richness and beauty, spiritual and musical. The illustrious names of Byrd, Lassus, Palestrina and Victoria, and their lesser contemporaries, illuminate the close of the greatest period of Catholic church music, a span of more than ten centuries, just as Johann Sebastian Bach's supreme art illuminates the close of the greatest period of Lutheran church music: while with Orlando Gibbons, last of the great Elizabethans, the finest period of polyphonic writing in the Anglican Church comes to an end.

From 1700 onward Catholic church music truly worthy of the liturgy appeared in ever decreasing quantity for reasons spiritual, the decline of faith: social, the increasing secularization of life: economic, the gradual loss of the patronage of the Church: artistic, the challenge to the forms which had held first place in the musical world, the Mass and Motet, by the instrumental and orchestral Sonata. These are matters that will naturally call for discussion in the course of this book. Meanwhile, one can wholeheartedly welcome the growing interest in the music of the Catholic Church brought about by the radio and the gramophone record, an interest naturally far more widespread than could have been the case before these inventions placed us in their debt. As Catholics we should feel ashamed that appreciation of our wonderful heritage of plainsong and polyphony is often found to be more marked in those musicians who are not of the household of the faith than in ourselves.

Some indeed of the musicologists, particularly the younger ones, who have contributed, or are contributing, notably to our knowledge of the great past are either not practising Christians, or perhaps not even Christians at all. Nevertheless, their interest in Catholic church music is not wholly aesthetic; their spirits also are touched. There are times when one is tempted to say of them, to quote St Augustine, *Multi sunt intus qui videntur esse foras* ("Many who appear to be without are within"). In this short book it will not be possible to discuss in any detail the huge array of composers and works that confront the author: many of them, indeed, must go without mention, and those that are mentioned will, for obvious reasons, tend to be those that are most familiar to the ordinary music lover. To proceed otherwise would provide merely a *catalogue raisonné,* whereas an outline of trends of thought and changing techniques will, it is to be hoped, prove of greater value in the space available.

The enormous quantity of music inspired by the liturgy of the Latin Church has made it necessary for the author to interpret the title of this small book strictly: even so he is conscious of many omissions.

Some of the judgements made in the book, particularly of the so-called baroque period and of the church music of the succeeding centuries, will not commend themselves to non-Catholics—for whom this book is not primarily intended—and may even be disturbing to Catholics who have not studied carefully the pronouncements of a long line of popes on church music, and the ideals it should follow: ideals which have recently been finely set out in detail in *Musicae Sacrae Disciplina* of Pius XII (1955) and in the *Instruction of the Sacred Congregation of Rites* (1958).[1] These form, with the

[1] *Sacred Music and Liturgy,* translated with an introduction and commentary by J. B. O'Connell, Burns & Oates, 1959.

Motu Proprio, a juridical code which is intended to have a binding force but which, when understood, leaves the composer with all the freedom he could justly claim if he believes music to be the handmaid of the liturgy and that, first and foremost, it is the Mass that matters.

CHAPTER I

PRE-CHRISTIAN SACRED MUSIC

THE NATURE OF CATHOLIC MUSIC

Musical sounds, however ordered, cannot of their nature be denominational. Our music is Catholic not by origin but by destination. It is conditioned by the liturgy and it is the hand-maid of the liturgy. Though the Church went singing into the world from her foundation, music is to her not an absolute necessity but a most beautiful and desirable embellishment; an addition which ought to be a great aid to worship but, as music is uneasy in a subordinate position and struggles to be autonomous, may also prove to be a considerable distraction. One reason for the constant and perhaps tiresome emphasis laid in this book upon the necessity of church music observing liturgical ideals is that the misdirected use of its sensuous appeal, with the sacred words as a peg, can induce an evanescent emotion that can only be described as *religioso* and of no spiritual benefit. We shall hear what the Fathers of the Church, the popes and the saints, have to say about that. There can be no question at all, when the nature and purpose of the liturgy is fully understood, that the music which spiritually, aesthetically and practically consorts most closely with the sacred words of the Catholic liturgies is plainsong, however unpopular this conclusion may be. We must, therefore, consider how Christian chant came into being and this will require a brief consideration of pre-Christian religious music.

Ethnology, defined by the *Oxford English Dictionary* as the "science of races and their relations to one another and characteristics", is an important part of comparative music-ology in so far as it concerns the study of primitive music. We learn from this study of traditions still alive today that there is indeed nothing new under the sun. Music, as Professor Marius Schneider writes in a brilliant chapter on the subject in the first volume of *The New Oxford History of Music,*

> is to a much greater extent than art bound up with everyday life (of primitive peoples) and with many special factors: psychological, sociological, religious, symbolic and linguistic. . . . Primitive man sings only when he has something to express. Since his singing is the spontaneous expression of his thought, song and speech are often mingled in the course of his perform-ance. If one tries to introduce a primitive man to a new tune (without the foreign words which he cannot understand) he will never stop asking what the song is about. For him the thoughts expressed in the song are at least as important as the melody itself.

This latter point is by no means universally true of the art-song, or indeed of the popular song, of our time where tune, rhythm (or the reverse), words is frequently the order of appeal: but it is, as we know, pre-eminently true of plainsong in which the word is the inspiring factor.

Primitive man makes no distinction between "religious" and "secular" music because, as Professor Schneider remarks, his "whole thinking is essentially religious or magical". The alliance of religious music, *per se,* and magic persisted in high civilizations at least as far down as the fourteenth cen-tury when the famous antiphon *Media vita in morte sumus* (often wrongly attributed to Notker) to which I shall return later, was forbidden by one of the Councils to be sung except by permission of the local bishop, as it had been used as an incantation or an imprecation.

The preconditions of the musical art are to be found in the oldest cultures, including much with which we are familiar in plainsong, "a mastery and more or less conscious shaping of the medium of expressing, collective performance but also a distinction between soloist and chorus, free as well as strict rhythm, and simultaneous singing, with canon as one of its oldest patterns, and with the frequent alternation of those very intervals favoured by the early forms of polyphony in the Church, unison, octave, fifth and fourth". It is outside the Church, therefore, as scholars have now come to believe, that we have to look for the origins of polyphony. Professor Schneider concludes his chapter with these striking words: "No art fascinates primitive man more than music: he is as vividly aware of its dynamic fluctuations between light and darkness as he is of the mysterious relationship between life and death."

The idea of music as more than music haunts the ancient East. In China its essence was held to be not sound but a transcendent power, its sound magically sustaining or, if improperly used, destroying universal harmony: and in India music is considered to bestow liberation, to serve to break the cycle of birth, death and rebirth, and to lead to ultimate bliss. Keats' well-known lines "Heard melodies are sweet but those unheard are sweeter" derives from the Indian and also the Greek philosophy of unmanifested sound, considered as identical with the divine creative principle of the Universe, a view held, as we shall see, by many Christian mystics and saints. Again we find that the modal system of the Indian ragas, though much more complex in use, has a certain affinity with the modes of the Eastern and Western Churches in its relative position of tones and semitones centring round a final and a dominant, though ragas are rather melody-types than modes. But it was also out of melody-types in Gregorian chant that the modal system, which postdates it, was deduced.

It is exciting to find the Mesopotamian liturgy, according to Stephen Langdon, had "the greatest system of musical ritual in any ancient religion" and that although we know little of the actual music used, "there have come down to us ... vast treasures by way of liturgies, breviaries, psalms and songs . . . a full index of this musical material would rival that of the Roman or Anglican books of devotion". Apparently the Mesopotamians "knew the penitential psalm, the antiphon, the precentor, incense and the *mater dolorosa*".[1]

Ancient Egypt had its college of priests in each temple for their "enchanting" music, a phrase, which we unthinkingly use, meant literally. St Clement of Alexandria, in a description of the divine books of the Egyptian liturgy, speaks of "ten books devoted to hymns, prayers, processions, festivals, first fruits and other constituent parts of temple worship". A large amount of liturgical material has been translated and one can see on the spot in the wonderful wall paintings, or in excellent reproductions, the details of the religious life and practice in ancient Egypt. As in the case of Mesopotamia we have the instruments used but no knowledge of the actual music: but it was thrilling to hear, after thousands of years, a silver and a copper trumpet from the tomb of Tutankhamen blown, in the resounding spaces of the Cairo Museum, by an English military bandsman.

HEBREW SACRED MUSIC

Jubal is mentioned in Genesis (4. 21) as "the founder of all those who play music, on the harp or the pipe", and in 31. 27 of the same book Laban is described as saying to his nephew Jacob, "I could have sped thee on thy way with good cheer, with singing, and music of timbrel and harp". In the

[1] *New Oxford History of Music*, Vol. I, "The Music of Ancient Mesopotamia", by Henry George Farmer, pp. 233–4.

case of Mesopotamia and Egypt we have at least specimens or portrayals of the actual instruments used but not one of those mentioned in the Bible has ever come to light. This, however, is not of great importance since their prototypes are familiar: the serious thing is the lack of any knowledge of the actual melodies used, or even of which and how many of the lyric pieces scattered through the various books were meant to be sung. It would be exciting if the caves in the Dead Sea area yielded up some evidence of musical notation though anything of the kind found might prove as frustrating as the Mesopotamian cuneiform tablets (c. 800 B.C.) which some musicologists believe to present musical notation, but which have defeated all attempts to penetrate their secrets.

It is not in doubt that instruments were used in the ceremonial of the Temple, for we have the violent utterance of the prophet Amos (5. 23): "I am sick and tired of . . . your solemn feasts; . . . O to be rid of the singing, the harp's music, that dins my ear!"

The first Temple, dating from the reign of Solomon (c. 970–933 B.C.) was destroyed by the Babylonians in 586 B.C., the second was begun, after the captivity, sixty-six years later, and we learn from 2 Paralipomena (5. 12–13) that vocal and instrumental music became more elaborate than before. "Once the place of music in the order of worship had been established, the development of musical *propria* for the daily and the festival services was inevitable . . . the Psalter (Pss. 92 and 30)[2] reflects the beginning of this development."[3] Many of the titles with which the psalms are headed remain obscure.

MUSIC AND THE SYNAGOGUE

We are here, however, particularly concerned, in this account of the background to Christian music, with the ser-

[2] The numbering of the psalms throughout is that of the Vulgate.
[3] *Op. cit.*, Vol. I, "Music in the Bible", by Carl H. Kraeling and Lucetta Mowry, p. 298.

vices of the synagogue and the extent to which music entered into· them, for this has a direct bearing on the origins of Christian chant. Synagogues were instituted as regular places for worship after the Babylonian exile of the sixth century when the dispersed Jews could not worship at the Temple. The worship, unlike that of the Temple, was non-sacrificial, and in the early period there were many varieties of it. It came to include prayers, psalm-singing of a responsorial character (e.g. the Hallel group of psalms (113–118) and doxologies attached to Pss. 41, 121. 18–19 etc.).

We do not, unfortunately, know whether the Jews of the Dispersion, who used the Greek version of the Scriptures, sang their "hymns and songs" to the melodic formulas they remembered or to the Greek modes, but it is certain that the music of the early synagogue, and thereafter, was exclusively vocal, "whether because of opposition to pagan custom or as a sign of mourning for the destruction of the Temple".[4]

The synagogue or "the little sanctuary", "an informal lay-men's institution", was influenced in some respects by the Temple liturgy and came to employ a professional cantor and though the earliest Hebrew melodies date only from the twelfth century, scholars have found what they regard as convincing evidence of earlier sources in the living tradition of the Georgian, Persian, Yemenite and Babylonian Jews which were remote from European Hebrew groups. It is noteworthy that though the secular music of these oriental Jews shows the common characteristics of their Christian or Mohammedan neighbours in their religious song, the cantillation of the· Bible, and the various liturgical units of synagogal worship, they were quite uninfluenced by their age-long proximity to differing systems and know of no sacred song built on the favourite oriental scale, the so-called Hedjaz mode, which points to a high antiquity in their chant. Later research has

[4] *Op. cit.*

simply confirmed the link between the chants they have preserved and Christian plainsong. Inflected monotone, psalmody with congregational refrains, jubilation (as in the plainsong Alleluia), a style dignified and distinguished from secular music, these were all features of synagogal worship that must have been familiar to our Lord and his disciples, and doubtless they would go to the Temple on important feast days as we, in a city, would go to a cathedral rather than a parish church.

CHAPTER II

PRE-GREGORIAN,

GREGORIAN AND OTHER

CHRISTIAN CHANT

THE CONSECRATION OF CHRISTIAN MUSIC

The Gospels tell us that at the end of the Last Supper our Lord and his disciples sang a hymn and then went out to the Mount of Olives. At this profoundly solemn moment tradition affirms that they sang the Hallel group of psalms (113–128) which were recited or sung at the principal Jewish festivals, and so at the Passover. In the apocryphal Acts of St John (second century)[1] there is a remarkable description of the hymn sung which does not accord with the above tradition. (Jesus) "bade us therefore make as it were a ring, holding one another's hands, and himself standing in the midst he said: 'Answer Amen unto me.' He began to sing a hymn and to say 'Glory be to thee, Father' and we, going about in a ring, answered him: Amen." The hymn and round dance concludes:

> Grace danceth. I would pipe: dance ye all. Amen.
> I would mourn: lament ye all. Amen.
> The Eight singeth praise with us. Amen.

[1] See Volume 72 in this series, p. 170.

The Twelve danceth on high. Amen.

The Whole on high hath part in our dancing. Amen.

Whoso danceth not, knoweth not what cometh to pass. Amen.[2]

Among the three versions of this cryptic and surely Gnostic text there is one in Latin transmitted by St Augustine, and it was set, in English, to music in our day by Gustav Holst, who, it may be remembered, quotes the plainsong hymns *Vexilla Regis* and *Pange lingua gloriosi* in his score of *The Hymn of Jesus*.

One may, perhaps, be allowed—with a measure of poetic licence—to consider that the singing at the Last Supper epitomized the consecration of the art of music to his Church by Christ.

The Acts of the Apostles show them and the ever increasing number of converts to Christianity continuing to worship in the Temple and the synagogue; the Christian synaxis, or non-Eucharistic service, was freely modelled on the pattern of synagogal worship, as we can see from the description of it given in the *Apology* of Justin Martyr.

Inevitably the converts drew away from Jewish places of worship to those of their own founding, the "home-churches" —the earlier synagogues had the same prefix—private houses of the wealthier members among them with former Jewish precentors to take charge of the proceedings. The extent of the link between synagogal and early Christian worship has sometimes been questioned on the grounds of St Paul's hatred of Jewish law: but when he exhorted the faithful in the Epistle to the Colossians to offer to the Lord "psalms, hymns and spiritual songs", and when he writes (in 1 Cor. 14. 26) "when you meet together each of you with a psalm to sing, or some doctrine to impart, a revelation to give, or ready to speak in strange tongues", we cannot accept that he expected the converts from Jewry to deny themselves their ancient and

[2] *The Sacred Bridge,* Eric Werner, pp. 208 ff.

hallowed chants, but he was also addressing the Gentiles, who knew no such music. It is obvious that there was much improvisation at these assemblies, that some members would be moved by the Holy Spirit to "testify", and that folk-songs might have been adapted to the song of praise or hymn sung. Greek was the liturgical language of the Roman Church up to the second half of the fourth century and some of the fragments of hymns in the New Testament (Ephes. 5. 14: 1 Tim. 3. 16 and 6. 15) are based not only on Jewish but also on Hellenic-oriental models. It is impossible to say what direct influence Greco-Roman music had on the Church's plainsong and the only document we have to estimate it is the so-called Oxyrhynchus hymn written in c. A.D. 300. This is the oldest piece of ecclesiastical music, the close of a hymn to the Holy Trinity by a Greek-speaking Christian in Egypt, and the music is set down in Greek alphabetical notation. Dr Wellesz points out that the melody is built up of a group of formulas in a way characteristic of Semitic melody–construction (and of Christian chant) and is not to be found in ancient Greek music.

With the gradual fusion, from the fourth century, of the Synaxis with the Eucharist, the distinctive Christian service, until they became the inseparable parts of a single rite: and with the observance of "hours" of prayer, of which we shall speak shortly, we have the foreshadowing of the eventual shapes of the Roman Mass and the Divine Office.

Before the persecution of the Christians was brought to an end by Constantine's Edict of Milan (A.D. 313) there could be no question of formal liturgical rites, regulated by authority, and our knowledge of music used at the gatherings of the early Christians is necessarily scanty. It might indeed be summed up in St Paul's exhortation in the passages from St Paul's Epistles already quoted and, as regards "psalms, hymns and spiritual songs" defined as (1) cantillation of the Jewish psalms, canticles and doxologies, (2) hymns similar to the fragments noted in the Acts of the Apostles with each word sung to one or two notes of the melodies, (3) Alleluias, florid melodies—perhaps of a highly emotional or exultant character—such as were sung in the Temple or synagogue.

For the rest an occasional testimony reaches us from other sources. Pliny reports to the Emperor Trajan in a famous letter (c. A.D. 112) that he hears of "Christians singing songs to Christ, addressing him as God". Tertullian, African Church Father (c. 160–c. 220) makes some references to antiphonal recitation or singing and the Jewish writer Philo (c. 20 B.C.– c. A.D. 50) in his report on the *Therapeutae*, a pre-Christian monastic community of Egyptian Jewish ascetics, describes antiphonal singing as one of their religious practices—this being its first mention in the Christian era.

The freedom of worship Constantine's Edict allowed to the Christian Church, and his conversion, made possible the construction of large basilicas at Jerusalem, Rome, Antioch, Alexandria and elsewhere, and the development in them of an ordered liturgy and its music—inseparably bound up together—and it also brought about the rise and swift development of monasticism.

"The liturgical forms", Peter Wagner writes, "quickly developed and an artistic psalmody spread over the world." We now begin to get vivid pictures of the Christian musical life of the time and of the enormous part the psalms played in it. Thus Eusebius (260–340) bishop of Caesarea writes:

The command to sing psalms in the name of the Lord was obeyed by everyone in every place: for the command to sing psalms is in force in all Churches which exist among the nations, not only for the Greeks but also for the Barbarians, throughout the whole world, in towns and villages and in the fields also, in short, in the whole Church the people of Christ, who are gathered from all nations sing hymns and psalms with a loud voice, so that the voice of the psalm singers is heard by those standing outside.

The bishop may exaggerate but his enthusiasm is infectious. It must, however, be said that the Church Fathers expressed strong disapproval of women's voices being loudly raised during the services. We can be sure that the chants the people sang were of a very simple character and that the number of psalms they knew by heart was not large: but they could all, without difficulty, join in refrains, Amen—Alleluia—or "For his mercy endureth for ever", sung between each verse of a psalm. For this purpose congregations, led by cantors, were divided into alternating choruses, each verse (when they knew the psalm as a whole) from either side being followed by the refrain, or antiphon, sung by all. The monk Cassian (360–450) tells us that in Gaul about 420, all the people joined in the "small doxology", that is, the *Gloria patri*.

A detailed account of liturgical observances in Jerusalem from Christmas to Whitsuntide was written for the benefit of her community by the Spanish Abbess Etheria in her book *Pilgrimage of Etheria* (385–8) which deals with her visits to the holy places of the East. She describes the regular singing of hymns and psalms, antiphons at Matins, psalms and hymns at the sixth and ninth hours, psalms, antiphons and hymns (suitable to the day and place) at Vespers, and mentions also that "it was customary to translate the lessons, where they were read in Greek, into Syriac and Latin for the benefit of those who did not understand that language".

This is a reminder that the transition from Greek to Latin as liturgical language took place between 360 and 382. The greater part of the Christian population in Rome had been of Greek-oriental descent and so the liturgy had, of course, to be celebrated in Greek. The growth of the Christian population in the fourth century made it imperative to use Latin, the language of the Roman-born converts but, as we know from the Trisagion sung on Good Friday (in the *Improperia*), Greek persisted in bilingual singing at important feasts. The Epistle and Gospel are, to this day, chanted first in Greek, and then in Latin at papal Masses. Professor Wellesz has shown in his valuable book *Eastern Elements in Western Chant* how the process of adapting the melodies to Latin texts was carried out. Much research, as he says, remains to be done in order to discover which melodies belong to the oldest layer and which, from the beginning, were written to Latin texts. There did exist, he stresses, an old layer of liturgical melodies that was introduced in the first centuries into the West by Christian missionaries and traders from the East, and this confirms the Syro-Palestinian and ultimately Jewish origin of Western chant.

At this point we should remind ourselves that everything came from the East. This is finely summarized by F. van der Meer in his *Atlas of Western Civilization*:

> The faith itself, the first theology, the "angelic" life of the monks, the devotion to the cross and the Mother of God. Were not the Byzantines the direct heirs of Paul and John, whose letters were still heard in the original language by the same congregations to whom they were originally addressed? Did not the majority of the bishoprics, and especially the most ancient, lie in the East? And where did the christianization of the world begin? In the East, the land of the Holy Places, of the Desert Fathers, of the Apologists, of the Councils, of the majestic liturgies, and of the decisive victories of orthodoxy over the Gnostic and christological heresies. To be sure, they had certainly accepted, first in their hearts and then with their lips, the prerogatives of Rome, the first apostolic see, and home of the innumerable martyrs whose graves lay like a wreath about her walls, but Rome had been abandoned by the emperor and thrice plundered by the Barbarians. Always threatened, and totally impoverished, she was soon to become a far off city, great only in her monuments, her memories, and by the presence of the successors of St Peter. In the sixth century she came under the jurisdiction of the Byzantine Church of Ravenna, but eventually the Holy See, the independent summit of the Church, escaped completely from the Greek *basileus*,

and by what in Greek eyes seemed an act of treacherous desertion, turned herself towards the West, and even toward the ruler of the barbaric Franks.

Roman sobriety has overlaid the Eastern elements in Western chant but they are nevertheless the underlay, and still easily perceptible, especially in the melismatic chants.

THE FATHERS OF THE CHURCH AND PLAINSONG

We have to bring to the study of plainsong both of East and West not only imagination but historical understanding. If the Fathers of the Church, a wonderful assemblage of great men, had not relentlessly opposed themselves to the secular music of their time the great art of plainsong, the triumph of the spiritual ideal in music, could not have come into being.

The antithesis between secular music and the kind of music felt suitable for Christian worship was pronounced. It provided problems which had to be resolved on religious, moral and aesthetic grounds, in that order: and the compromise that had to be made eventually did not come about until the golden age of plainsong, the sixth to the eighth century, had passed. The Church was then left in possession of a rich treasure which she declares to represent the highest spiritual ideals to which music can attain.

The virtues of nobility, tranquillity, solemnity, restraint and so forth, were certainly not to be found, or expected, in the secular music which many of the converts to Christianity had frequented with clear consciences while still pagans and which were now to be forbidden to them. The Fathers were well aware of the power for evil of this debased music, and even more of the words and actions with which it was associated, but they were as aware of the compelling power for good of truly spiritual music. They were greatly influenced by the teaching of the Greek philosophers and their schools, many of whose ideas they adopted. Between music and piety,

Diogenes had affirmed, there was an indissoluble bond: a view also held by Plotinus, who held that the knowledge of beauty must serve to purify the soul and deliver it from worldly elements. Nearly all these philosophers, indeed, expounded the ethical view of music. Plato is severe on those who judge music by the pleasure taken in listening to it, a theme on which St Augustine enlarges in a passage in his *Confessions*, too well known to quote. The Fathers also followed Aristotle in believing that musical compositions reproduce states of the soul. It is easy, therefore, to understand their frequent references to the story of David driving evil spirits out of Saul with music. If music had such spiritually curative power, how important, they argued—forgetting perhaps the unfortunate effect David's playing once had on Saul—it is to decide what music is pernicious and what of service, in order to be able to fight the first and develop the second.

Every musician today is aware of the morally debilitating elements in popular music and of how mistaken are those who wish, with a sincere intention, to introduce the idioms of such music into the Church to draw the people in. They will be able, therefore, to sympathize with the views of the early Fathers on the kind of music Christians heard, unavoidably, in the pagan schools in which they went to study and, avoidably if with difficulty, at parties or in the theatres, and they did not mince their words. "It must be banned," cries St Clement of Alexandria († *c.* 215), "this artificial music which injures souls and draws them into various states of feelings, snivelling, impure, and sensual, even a bacchic frenzy and madness. One must not expose oneself to the powerful character of exciting and languorous modes, which by the curves of their melodies lead to effeminacy and infirmity of purpose. Let us leave coloured (chromatic) harmonies to banquets where no one even blushes at music crowned with flowers and harlotry." Reading this modern man may think darkly of Freud: but Clement was a sane and well-balanced person, untroubled by a past history like St Augustine's and not at all opposed to the serious practice of the arts of poetry and music.

St John Chrysostom (*c.* 347–407) is another equally sane critic of pagan music and he knew, also, that a feeling for music was innate in human beings. He recalls how nurses soothe infants with lullabies, riders urge on their horses with songs, peasants, husbandmen and sailors ease their work with rhythmical cries and songs, and so on. But while appreciating such natural manifestations he had at heart, in common with all the Fathers of the Church, a music that would serve "for the glory of God and the propagation of the divine word".

"It must be submitted", he wrote, "to severe control: and everything must be banished which recalls the cult of pagan gods and the songs of actors." For this reason purists frowned on the use of florid melody—as in an Alleluia—and with ample reason, as we shall see, where solo singers of the chant were concerned. Instruments, also, or at least those used in the theatre or at banquets, were proscribed. Clement has another ground of complaint: "We have need of only one instrument, the word of peace, and not the psaltery nor the trumpet, the cymbals, the 'flute' [the *aulos*—a double reed instrument] beloved of those who go to battle." But he allows for the use of lyre or cither at private gatherings.

A number of Christians used these instruments and for a time they and others were even introduced into certain churches. To this day rattles and drums accompany Ethiopian chant, but mainly for the purpose of emphasizing the rhythm of the dance undertaken by two or three priests in the middle of a circle of priests and deacons. This liturgical dance, adopted also by the Coptic Church, comes from Egypt where it was witnessed and roundly condemned by Clement of Alexandria during his stay there. What then, some musicians no doubt asked, of the command in the Old Testament to praise God with harps, psalteries, trumpets and cymbals: above all, what about David dancing before the Lord?

Instead of pointing to the contemporary abuse of instruments or developing the idea of a more spiritual music to be played on them, the Fathers resorted to a great deal of poetical but rather tortuous symbolism such as the statement that the ten-stringed psaltery was a symbol of the ten commandments. Such evasion was unnecessary. The opposed fields of sacred and profane music were clear enough. The moral effect of church music was to elevate the soul: of theatre music to titillate the senses. Sacred music, as they said, should lead to purity not obscenity, sobriety not drunkenness, to virility not effeminacy; and the end of music, for Christians, was to further the contemplation and love of God. Such also was to be the spirit of its performance.

It may seem incredible to us, who know so little of the Psalter today, that anyone could claim for psalmody that

it calms the emotions, awakes courage, relieves grief, moderates the passions, drives away cares, consoles in affliction, leads sinners to repentance, provokes piety, peoples deserts, gives wise institutions to the State, founds converts, incites to a chaste life, teaches love of one's neighbour, praises charity, gives patience, affirms the Church, sanctifies the priest, banishes evil spirits, preaches the future, initiates us into the divine mysteries and preaches the Trinity.

Such was the pronouncement of Proclus, Bishop of Constantinople († 446). His account fills out in detail the fine saying of St Athanasius (296–373): "the words of this book [the Psalter] include the whole life of man, all conditions of the mind and movements of thought". In the following sentence from a spiritual tract he seems to be writing of private devotion: "At midnight thou shalt arise and sing praise to the Lord thy God. For in this same hour did our Lord rise from the dead, and sang praise to his Father. On this account it is ordained that we praise God at this hour. . . . Say as many psalms as thou canst say standing . . . after three psalms say Alleluia."

St Athanasius was a friend of St Antony of Egypt, usually spoken of as the founder of Christian monasticism, and it was one of his followers, the Abbot Pambo, who rebuked his monks for using melodious refrains "which cannot produce contrition and making the church and their cells resound with their voices as if they were a herd of bulls". The Fathers constantly insist that "we must sing to God more with the soul than with the voice" and warn singers against oiling their throats and larynxes with medicaments as actors do.

It seems to have been a constant struggle to get priests and congregations to behave with due reverence. The Council of Toledo (589) was compelled to legislate against the practice of dancing during services—the tradition survives in worthier form in the *Dance of the Seizes*, a religious dance by boys before the Blessed Sacrament every day in Seville Cathedral during the octaves of Corpus Christi and of the Immaculate Conception—or against the introduction of lewd songs during feasts celebrating the dedication of a church or in honour of a martyr. Priests had to be recalled to a sense of their dignity and not to listen to the songs of actors. The Council of Glasgow (747) decreed that priests must not adopt an effeminate pronunciation after the manner of poets in the world nor imitate the habits of tragedians and so draw attention away from the sacred words. They must pay heed to the simple and holy character of the chant, according to the traditions of the Church. Reading these constant complaints, repeated again and again through succeeding centuries, until the Counter-Reformation brought a salutary but costly shock, one sadly concludes that man is not naturally religious and urgently needs the grace of God to tread the narrow path.

We may fittingly end these citations from the Fathers of the Church with two beautiful passages. St Ambrose (*c.* 333–

397) in his commentary on Psalm 1 writes first critically, and then ardently:

What a labour it is to achieve silence in church while the lessons are being read. When one man would speak, the congregation make a disturbance. But when the psalm is read (i.e. sung) it makes its own "silence". Psalms are sung by emperors; the common people rejoice in them. Each man does his utmost in singing what will be a blessing to all. Psalms are sung in the home and rehearsed on the streets. A psalm is learnt without labour and remembered with delight. Psalmody unites those who disagree, makes friends of those at odds, brings together those who are out of charity with one another. Who could retain a grievance against the man with whom he had joined in singing before God? The singing of praise is the very bond of unity, when the whole people join in a single act of song. The strings of the harp are of varying lengths, but the harmony is a unity. The musician's fingers, too, may often make mistakes on the small strings, but in the congregation that great musician, the spirit, cannot err. Psalmody is the rewarding work of the night, the grateful relaxation of the busy day, the good beginning and the fortifying conclusion of all work. It is the ministry of the angels, the strength of the heavenly host, the spiritual sacrifice.

These glowing words echo those of the Bishop of Constantinople quoted on page 27.

The second passage is familiar but cannot be often enough repeated. St Augustine, warm-hearted as St Ambrose, his great friend, writes in his *Confessions* (IX. 6)

The days were not long enough as I meditated, and found wonderful delight in meditating, upon the depth of your design for the salvation of the human race. I wept at the beauty of your hymns and canticles, and was powerfully moved at the sweet sound of your Church's singing. These sounds flowed into my ears, and the truth streamed into my heart, so that my feeling of devotion overflowed, and the tears ran from my eyes, and I was happy in them.

It is true that St Augustine, in the succeeding chapter of his *Confessions*, mistrusted the emotional state described above and generated in the early days of his new faith, but he decided in favour of the custom of singing in church provided that the words that were sung should move the hearer more than the singing.

In the second half of the fourth century, when Latin superseded Greek as the language of the Roman Church, there appeared the Itala, or Old Latin, translation of the Greek Septuagint which was itself superseded by the Vulgate, a translation of the whole Bible, not only of the Old Testament, begun by St Jerome in 382 at the command of Pope Damasus and completed *c*. 404.

We have no knowledge as to what the original Roman chants, or those received by Rome from the Churches of Jerusalem, Antioch and other sources, were like, but the survival of the Itala text in Roman chant books is a valuable aid in the dating of the then existing melodies. Thus Isidore of Seville, in the first half of the seventh century, says the version of St Jerome, to be preferred to the earlier one, "is already in use in all the churches".

We come now to the difficult and much debated question of the part St. Gregory (540–604: pope from 590) took in the reform of the chant associated with his name. It rests on a venerable tradition, unchallenged till the seventeenth century. Thus in 789 the Emperor Charlemagne ordered Gallican authority "To return to the fountain-head of St Gregory, since you have clearly debased the ecclesiastical chant", and tried to impose Gregorian chant throughout the West. It was, however, John the Deacon in a chapter of his *Life of St Gregory* (*c*. 872), nearly 300 years after the pope's death, who gave widespread currency to the existence of a *Cento Antiphonarius* (a "patchwork" of Mass chants) compiled by St Gregory, and this led to a large number of pictorial representations of

Gregory sitting on the papal throne with a dove perched on his shoulder whispering into his ear. In some of these a scribe has made a hole in the curtain hiding the pope from him and is observing the spectacle described.

It seems incontrovertible that Gregory did play some part in the reform of the chant and certain that he reorganized the song school at Rome: the "whip of correction" is indeed preserved as a relic in his church on the Coelian Hill at Rome. Song schools had been in existence since Pope Leo I († 461), and it was from these schools that singers went out as musical missionaries to spread knowledge of the Roman chant. Thus in 680 Benedict Biscop, returning to England from Rome, took with him a skilled singer to teach the monks of Wearmouth Abbey the system of singing as it was practised at St Peter's: and it was, of course, with Roman chant that St Augustine of Canterbury and his band of monks greeted the Anglo-Saxons when he landed at Kent in the summer of 597 bringing with him, according to Egbert, Bishop of York (c. 732), Gregory's "book of chants and prayers". The Venerable Bede in his *Ecclesiastical History of the English People* (completed in 731) praises Bishop Putta of Rochester for his knowledge of the Roman chant which "he had learnt from the pupils of St Gregory", and there are other similar references. If the *Cento Antiphonarius* attributed to St Gregory came to light with some kind of musical notation we should be spared much disputation. As it is the earliest noted manuscripts, apart from some fragments, that have come down to us, are of the ninth century and these being staffless cannot be read except, where possible, when compared with the manuscripts of the eleventh century, which, having staff lines, show exact intervals.

St Gregory, therefore, could only revise what was handed down by oral tradition and that, unless some form of notation unknown to us existed, would appear to indicate that the melodies of his time were of a simple character and few in number. In a revealing discussion of the subject, in his book *Gregorian Chant*, Dr Apel asserts that it cannot be maintained that the melodies are as old as the texts and feasts, the former dating back, as far as we know, to the middle of the eighth century, the latter at least to the time of St Gregory. "It is", he says, "a matter of scientific caution and prudence to assign to the liturgical melodies, as we have them, a considerably later date than has generally been done before."

Moreover, the term Gregorian chant is a misnomer. The chant came from such places in West Europe as St Gall, Einsiedeln, Metz, Chartres, Laon and Montpellier, that is from the Franco-Germanic Empire, in addition to Roman sources. In his great work on *The Mass of the Roman Rite*, Fr J. A. Jungmann writes: "About the middle of the tenth century the Roman liturgy began to return in force from Franco-Germanic lands to Italy and to Rome, but it was a liturgy which meanwhile had undergone radical changes and a great development. This importation entailed supplanting the local form of the Roman liturgy by its Gallicized version, even at the very centre of Christendom."

The melodies must have been profoundly affected by these developments. One can assume that the simplest ones have preserved their primitive character but that the ornate chants are, as we have them today, Franco-Roman products of the eighth and ninth centuries.

It most certainly cannot be said that St Gregory had no interest in the chant on the grounds, for example, that he forbade deacons to ascend the ambo and sing the Gradual. This was, especially in its verse, a chant requiring a highly skilled performer, and as we know singers are prone to vanity. The young men, with their carefully oiled hair and silk robes appear to have been prima donnas and St Gregory rightly considered that their exhibitionism was endangering their souls. The verse of the Gradual for the second Sunday after

Epiphany (*Confiteantur Domino*) might well have been composed by one of these deacons, with the object of showing off how he could negotiate a slow trill. At the same time Tracts, Graduals and verses of the Alleluia, and some Offertories, do indeed require good vocalization to bring out their fine points.

The elements of St Gregory's *Cento Antiphonarius* are practically unchanged today, though certain additions and eliminations were made in later centuries. The contents of the collection consist of direct psalmody: 23 Tracts; responsorial psalmody: 110 Graduals, 100 Alleluias; antiphonal psalmody: 150 Introits, 102 Offertories, 150 Communions. As has been said, this large collection of liturgical pieces may well have been sung to comparatively few chants but with the development of the song schools and above all with the possibility of noting down the music, even before the invention of the stave, the chants would naturally have increased in number and complexity. It took the singers nearly ten years to learn the repertory by heart: for even when the music could be written down much of it had to be sung from one large book, illuminated by a smoky lamp for the cantors but leaving the rest of the choir in comparative darkness.

Gregorian chant, to use the traditional if inaccurate term, is "the most complete treasure of antiquity bequeathed to us by any art", and as has been said before, it is on practical, aesthetic and spiritual grounds the only perfect liturgical music. Regarded aesthetically it prefigures many developments in Western music; the *da capo* aria (as in a *Kyrie, Sanctus-Benedictus* or *Agnus Dei*, the *Alleluia* and—if the repeat were made as it used to be—the *Gradual,* the leading motive as in the antiphon for the Vespers of Christmas Day *Hodie Christus natus est,* and other *Hodie* antiphons, the building to a climax as in the verse of the Gradual for Epiphany *Surge et illuminare* or the soaring *Jubilate* for the second Sunday after Epiphany, the rondo forms of the short or great responsories. Here we find, also, the instinctive sense of style that leads the composer to ornament a cadence—as in the final petition of most of the Kyries—the coloratura kind of writing that later flourished in opera, above all a marriage of word and tone that is unequalled in the song literature of the world, Purcell or Wolf or Britten notwithstanding. Today the Mass means to most people the Ordinary, or unvarying part. This is actually the last section of the *Graduale Romanum*, properly to be known as the *Kyriale* and only in modern times incorporated into the *Graduale*. Some of the melodies in it, the simpler ones such as Mass XVIII, are very ancient, and many of them, such as Mass XI (*Orbis factor*) have a folk-song like, popular, appeal. They were meant for congregational singing but became eventually too elaborate for the purpose and were taken over by the choir. As early as the fourth century the Council of Laodicea had forbidden all but specifically designated singers to take part in the singing, so that it should be on the level of the other arts pressed into the service of the Church, and we are only just now recovering the practice of congregational singing of the Ordinary.

The laity have long neglected the beautiful service of Vespers and in many places also ignore the equally beautiful service of Compline—the perfect end to Sunday observance. They need to be reminded that the ideal of the Christian life in the ancient Church was "a constant communion with God, maintained by as frequent prayer as possible, prayer both in assembly and in private".

In the fourth century private prayers said at dawn, at midday and in the evening, were adopted by monastic communities, as the Spanish Abbess Etheria found in the course of her pilgrimage to the Holy Places. She heard the Offices, as they were called, being recited in the Church of the Holy Sepulchre at Jerusalem. The people came to demand that the clergy should continue to observe these hours of prayer, even if they themselves were not present: and this observance in its final form of the Divine Office became, and has remained, obligatory on most conventual communities of men and women, and on the secular clergy. The singing of the entire Psalter was the main purpose of this kind of worship and St Benedict (c. 480–c. 550) lays down, in his monastic Rule, a plea for carrying this through weekly in the Divine Office, the *Opus Dei*—to which, he says, nothing is to be preferred.

Matins, the long night office (originally Vigils) was followed by Lauds, sung originally at dawn, and Prime, the first of the day hours, was sung an hour after sunrise. Terce, Sext and None, the "little" hours, followed about 9 a.m., midday and 3 p.m. respectively, and Vespers between 4 and 6 p.m. Vespers, the most ancient of all the hours, had its origin in the first part of the nocturnal vigils of the primitive Christian assembly, when the lamps were lit—hence its original title *Lucernarium.* St Benedict added Compline—really an eighth hour—when the whole monastic family gathered together in prayer before retiring, and the "great silence" fell upon the house.

The texts and music of the Office took shape much more slowly than those of the Mass and are still subject to modification and reform. The many books that contained the texts were eventually collected into the Breviary (the "abridgement") and the music into the *Antiphonale.*

The *Antiphonale Romanum* contains over 2,000 antiphons for use with the psalms and canticles. These antiphons, which in general, have their words taken from the psalms themselves are, musically, usually of a simple character. They give the mind a leading motive, related to the spirit of feria or feast, on which to meditate during the singing of the psalm and they also determine the mode of the psalm and its ending. The eight psalm tones and the *tonus peregrinus* (the "stranger" tone) never weary the ear—they are timeless. There is a story, perhaps *ben trovato,* of an Anglican vicar and his wife who were so enamoured of these tones that they used them to converse in them at breakfast! With an even rhythmic motion, like waves gently breaking on the shore, the tones pass from side to side of the choir in antiphonal chanting, and varied endings are provided to fit the antiphons.

It is sad that the many beautiful hymns in the Divine Office are so little known by Catholics. They are, like all hymns, strophic in form and variable in metre, but the majority are in the metre favoured by St Ambrose, who introduced hymns into the West. The Roman Church did not admit them into the secular Office until the twelfth century but St Benedict makes provision for them in his Rule, calling them by the general title of Ambrosianum. The Roman Church's prejudice against hymns was expressed in the earliest years of her existence and arose from a dislike of introducing other than biblical words in the liturgy and also from the fear of their being used as a vehicle for heretics to propagate errors, as Bardesanes (154–222) the father of Syrian hymnology so successfully did.

The hymns in the Roman Breviary known to be by St Ambrose are *Aeterna rerum Conditor* (Sunday, Lauds), *Splendor paternae gloriae* (Monday, Lauds) and *Aeterna Christi munera* (Common of many martyrs). He uses iambic dimetres (defined by St Augustine as a short and a long of three beats) and the swinging rhythm of the melodies to the hymns would account for their enormous popularity. He was, indeed, charged with "bewitching" the people with them—here, once more, we have a kind of magic in music, as in the pagan religions (see pp. 12–14). St Ambrose composed his first hymns for his people to sing, together with psalms, when they were guarding their church at Milan against the Arians, led by Empress Justina, so that they should not "pine away in the tediousness of sorrow". The siege over, he retained hymn singing in his services and it was imitated, as St Augustine says, "by almost all of thy congregations throughout the rest of the world".

It is not at all certain whether the existing melodies to the Ambrosian hymns are by the great bishop. As with all other hymns in the Roman liturgy they are not sung metrically: very often, indeed, the melodies ignore the metre, for accent was already replacing quantity in the time of St Ambrose.

The magnificent line of Latin hymn writers includes, in addition, Sedulius (ninth century), Venantius Fortunatus (c. 535–c. 600), Peter Abelard (1079–1142) and St Thomas Aquinas (1225–74). We owe to Fortunatus the splendid *Vexilla Regis prodeunt* ("The royal banners forward go") which he wrote for the reception of a fragment of the cross at Poitiers and which, five hundred years later, became the marching song of the Crusades, and *Pange, lingua, gloriosi lauream certaminis*; these two hymns are sung at Vespers, Matins and Lauds, respectively, during Passiontide and on the feast of the Exaltation of the Cross (September 14th). St Thomas Aquinas wrote all the hymns of the Corpus Christi Office, notably *Pange lingua gloriosi Corporis mysterium* sung at Vespers and at processions of the Blessed Sacrament. *Veni Creator Spiritus*, in use at ordinations in the eleventh century and since, is by an unknown author, and *Te Deum laudamus* (or at least that part of it up to *Aeterna fac cum sanctis tuis in gloria numerari*) is probably by St Niceta of Remesiana (335–415). We shall see how fruitfully the fine melodies of these hymns were used in later years.

The two great collections of Gregorian chant for Mass and the Divine Office and other services cover every phase of the Church's worship and form the largest assemblage of monophonic music in existence. It is music, therefore, that relies entirely on the single and, ideally, unaccompanied melodic line to express a wide variety of spiritual states and emotions. The music is the handmaid of the words, though in the long, florid and vocalized passages, such as the final vowel of the Alleluia, the music becomes for the moment autonomous. In similar passages built into a Gradual or an Offertory the chief accent of the word is often given to a single note or small group of notes with high melodic relief, the melismas being given to a succeeding vowel, on which the chief accent seems to shine down. The chant owes its flexibility to freedom from any regularly recurring "strong" accent, from anything—except in some hymns—approaching metrical accent.

This brings us to the vexed question of the rhythmic treatment of the chant. It is too technical a matter to deal with in any detail here but it may be said that there are two main schools of thought. The Solesmes school hold that though the rhythm conditioned by the text, with its principal and secondary accents, must be taken into account, so must also the rhythm inherent in the music, the two not always coinciding and so needing to be properly balanced: and that the beat in the chant, represented by the quaver as unit, is indivisible, though it may be lengthened. Binary and ternary groups of notes are mixed at will, producing the free rhythm, essentially a prose rhythm, that can make long stretches of unaccompanied melody acceptable to the ear. Solesmes insist that the sense of rhythm is awakened in the mind not only by stress but also by melodic elevation, and by lengthening of notes. Rhythm, in Dom Mocquereau's excellent definition, is essentially "the passage from movement to repose".

A sensation was caused by the publication, in 1958, of a book by a Dutch Jesuit, Fr J. A. W. Vollaerts,[3] who sought to prove, from a prolonged study lasting thirty years of the manuscripts and particularly of those called "rhythmic",[4] and from the writings of the theorists, that the rhythm of the chant was, and should be, metrical, there being short and long notes, quavers, so to speak, and crotchets, in due proportion.

[3] J. A. W. Vollaerts: *Rhythmic Proportions in Early Medieval Ecclesiastical Chant* (Leiden, 1958).

[4] That is, with letters such as *c* (*celeriter*), *t* (*tenere*), *m* (*mediocriter*) placed over some notes. These are variously interpreted as nuances, or as affecting the values of notes.

This sincere attempt, which met with approval in some quarters, hostility in others, has not been so far followed up with any positive results and may go the way of all other mensuralist theories of the past. The Solesmes method cannot be proved to be historically correct, but it can be heard to be aesthetically beautiful and spiritually satisfying.

EXPRESSION AND WORD PAINTING

There are few experiences in music more painful than hearing plainsong performed in a sluggish, unrhythmical manner and with little attention paid to clear and meaningful enunciation: and when so performed it is no wonder that the chant is written off as a dreary and unending kind of ululation. It is almost equally offensive to hear it given a romantic kind of expression or a dramatic emphasis foreign to it. As the Fathers of the Church rightly observed it must primarily be felt in the soul, and what moves the soul must be given sober and restrained expression, comparable to that of the words of the liturgy, by the voice. One can say without fear of contradiction that the singing of the psalms in choir needs no "expression" but merely one tone of voice whatever the nature of the psalm. It would be as theatrical to sing the *De profundis* softly as to sing *Laudate Dominum* loudly. For monks the singing of the psalms is a communal religious meditation and once the psalm or canticle is begun nothing should disturb its even tenor. The case, as regards the Office, differs to some extent with the antiphons: for while psalm singing is based on simple melodic formulas the antiphons are clothed in developed melody, as are the various pieces of the Proper of the Mass. What, in terms of expression, Gregorian chant means to a monk who has lived with it day and night during a long monastic life can best be appreciated by reading the comments of Dom Joseph Gajard, O.S.B., Choirmaster of St Pierre de Solesmes, in the booklet he compiled for the first set of gramophone records of his choir, or on the sleeves of subsequent single records made by it. To him each mode has its own *ethos*, each piece its own emotional climate: and he uses such adjectives as warm, virile, animated, harsh, serene, tranquil, caressing, humble, joyous, light and gay, climactic, graceful, intense, etc. to describe what he finds in the music and—one must again emphasize—what he feels in his soul. At the same time it cannot be denied that the unknown composers of the music itself were moved to "comment" melodically on this large gamut of emotions.

The *Salve Regina,* both in the solemn tone and the simple, and best known, tone ends with melodic phrases to the words *O clemens, O pia, O dulcis Virgo Maria* that exquisitely underline the loving tenderness of the words. To hear the solemn tone sung by a Cistercian community after Compline is an unforgettable experience, and one engendered not only by the environment but above all by the penetrating beauty of the words and music.

The closing phrases of *Ave verum* to the words *O Jesu dulcis, O Jesu pie, O Jesu fili Mariae* are equally moving: and what love breathes in the opening phrase of *Alma redemptoris Mater*! Such expressive phrases can be called word-painting, and examples of the kind are numerous. The Epiphany season offers three vivid illustrations. In the verse of the Gradual of the feast itself there is a soaring phrase on *illuminare (Surge et illuminare Jerusalem)* that is indeed an illumination and in the Offertory for the first Sunday after the Epiphany the second *Jubilate* goes up to heaven in a long and thrilling phrase, like the joyous sound of a trumpet whose fanfares it seems to imitate. (But that analogy is, one must admit, romantic.) The Communion chant of the second Sunday after Epiphany is a little drama in miniature. The words describe the miracle at Cana and at "Thou has kept the good wine till now" there is a high-flung phrase of joy, twice repeated, that not only illustrates the delight of the master of the feast but seems to indicate that whoever wrote the melody appreciated good wine! One can recall, also, the great cry from the Cross in the Good Friday Responsory *Tenebrae factae sunt, Deus meus ut quid me dereliquisti* ("My God why hast thou forsaken me"), words treated as a high point of climax. Less striking, but also dramatic, is the cry of *Adjuva nos Deus salutaris noster* in the Tract for Ash Wednesday placed high in the voice after a low-pitched section. The most remarkable example of all, and uncontrovertible evidence of deliberate dramatic underlining, comes in an Offertory verse, *Vir erat*,[5] long since out of use, which graphically describes Job, tormented by pain and anguish, crying out again and again to see "the good things" of his earlier days. The words "ut videat bona" are repeated no less than six times in phrases that reach a high emotional pitch.

It is easy to object that the Gregorian composers (a term they would not have recognized) sometimes set *ascendit* or *descendit* to phrases that correspond with the sense of the words, and sometimes to phrases that contradict it, and indeed, in adapted chants, often put phrases to words of very different significance to the originals. This proves nothing: the technique of adaptation was an accepted thing. We have to remember that a chorale such as *Jesu, meine Freude* was originally a secular love song, *Flora, meine Freude*. The melody is the same in each case, though certainly disposed in a different setting for use in church.

The liturgy is, as we know, meant for corporate, not personal and individual expression, but that is true of all choral singing and does not prevent the individual feeling the emotional or dramatic impact of what he sings, or the choirmaster speaking imaginatively of its presentation. The result will be a disciplined, and in the case of the liturgy, a restrained performance in which each voice will, to some extent, be coloured

[5] To be found in *Offertoriale, sive versus Offertoriorum*, edited by Carolus Ott.

by what it sings, but in which no one voice stands out. But the sensitive listener who knows the chant well will soon discern whether what is sung is truly being felt.

To the cantors, who are in fact soloists, a greater latitude is allowed, a latitude often abused in the past as we saw in St Gregory's strictures about deacons singing the Gradual, and many are the denunciations of vain singers down the years. Abbot Aelred writing in the twelfth century speaks of singers "whinnying like horses, using gestures, swaying their bodies, twisting their lips, and rolling their eyes", and Erasmus (1467–1536) about how "a set of creatures who should be bewailing their sins think to please God by gurgling in their throats".

The Fourth Council of Carthage ordered the following words to be spoken at the blessing of the canons, or singing men, in the newly formed schools of chant (fourth century): "See that thou believe in thy heart what thou singest with thy mouth, and approve in thy works what thou believest in thy heart", a blessing that has lost none of its relevance today. This section may fitly end with the beautiful words of St Bernard of Clairvaux (1090–1153).

> Let the chant be full of gravity; let it be neither worldly, nor too rude and poor. . . . Let it be sweet, yet without levity, and, while it pleases the ear, let it move the heart. It should alleviate sadness, and calm the angry spirit. It should not contradict the sense of the words, but rather enhance it. For it is no slight loss of spiritual grace to be distracted from the profit of the sense by the beauty of the chant, and to have our attention drawn to a mere vocal display, when we ought to be thinking of what is sung.

THE ORDINARY OF THE MASS

The plainsong most familiar to congregations is naturally that of the Ordinary and many of them have learnt to sing the

Missa de Angelis (VIII). These chants are given dates in the *Kyriale* in the *Graduale Romanum* (and the *Liber Usualis*) edited by the monks of Solesmes and it will be found, in the Mass just mentioned and in the rest, that the dates vary from section to section. Thus the *Kyrie* of VIII is dated fifteenth–sixteenth centuries, the *Gloria* sixteenth century, the *Sanctus* eleventh–twelfth centuries, and the *Agnus Dei* fifteenth century. The reason for these variations is that the present system of printing the Ordinary of the Mass as a cycle of chants is of modern origin. They were previously grouped together according to their categories: and even now the *Credo* settings are so grouped together in the *Graduale*. The earliest known settings are of the tenth century and the latest the seventeenth century, the most fruitful period being from the eleventh to the twelfth centuries. It is known that there exist about 200 melodies for the *Kyrie*, so that the twenty-nine settings in the Gradual (eighteen in organized Masses, the rest to be used *ad libitum*) represent only a very small portion of the total output. There is a distinctly popular flavour in many of the chants of the Ordinary that may reflect the influence of secular song.

The Encyclical of Pius XII, dated December 25th, 1955, directs that

everywhere throughout the world the following very easy Gregorian settings (of the Ordinary) are to be taught to the faithful: *Kyrie eleison, Sanctus-Benedictus* and *Agnus Dei*: from No. XVI of the Roman Gradual: *Gloria in excelsis Deo, Ite missa est—Deo gratias* from No. XV: also *Credo* I or III. By this means something very desirable will be attained, namely, that Christians throughout the whole world will be able to express their common faith by active participation in the most holy sacrifice of the Mass, and moreover, will be able to do this in one and the same joyful common song.

It is defeatism of the worst kind to suggest that this direction—one might indeed say this command—cannot be carried out. There will always be members of the congregation incapable of singing anything but the National Anthem, and that discordantly, but the great majority could easily learn the chants suggested by the Holy Father if given proper instruction and guidance by their parish priests or persons designated by them—choirmaster or organist.

TROPE AND SEQUENCE

It will be noticed that the chants of the Ordinary carry a subtitle, for example, *Kyrie fons bonitatis* (No. II) for solemn feasts. This is a reference to the practice of "troping" which became common from the ninth to the thirteenth centuries, and even later. To the existing *Kyrie* melody words were added, one syllable to one note, which made the melismatic melody syllabic. Thus *Kyrie, fons bonitatis Pater unigenite a quo bono cuncta procedunt, eleison.*

This practice needs explanation. It was an upsurge of creative activity in an age when the *corpus* of Gregorian chant was standardized and could not be supplanted. But the addition of words to an existing chant, or of music in a similar style, as for example the extending of the melisma or *jubilus* on the last vowel of the *Alleluia* or its repetition, was a way of amplifying the existing chant. It was never recognized as part of the official liturgy and seems to have been practised mainly in monasteries.

The origin of tropes is obscure, so obscure that it has been thought that some of the melodies of the *Kyries* of the Ordinary may have been at first independent compositions, before being deprived of their words and rendered melismatic.

The trope has been defined as "an amplification or embellishment or intercalation added in either words or music to a Gregorian chant used in the authorized liturgy and the Sequence (that which follows) is the special kind of trope which consists of words only, or of words and music, or of music only, in the melismas attached to the melody of an *Alleluia*". The theory that words were added to long melismas to help singers to memorize them may well be true but does not explain why wordless melodies were also added. Troping covered a large part of the liturgy but the most abiding form of it, the most artistic, was that of the kind called Sequence. This was not the invention of the Notker Balbulus (the stammerer), a monk of St Gall, as has often been said. Some time towards the end of the ninth century a monk, fleeing from the Abbey of Jumièges (near Rouen), which had been sacked by the Normans, came to St Gall, bringing with him an antiphonary which contained verses set to the *Jubili* (or *Sequentiae*) of the *Alleluia*. Notker improved on these and the result is shown in his famous collection of 115 Sequences, of which about 46 are ascribed to himself.

The original Sequences were non-metrical, with lines of varying length, and a pattern developed of melodies set to pairs of verses which remained a characteristic of the Sequence. One of these, *Laetabundus*, became the model for a hundred or so imitations. It has a refrain at the end of most of the double versicles. The two chief schools of Sequence-writing were St Gall and St Martial, German and Anglo-French respectively, but Sequence-writing attained its highest point in the compositions of Adam, a monk in the Abbey of St Victor, outside Paris, whose texts are both metrical and rhythmic.

The beautiful Easter Sequence *Victimae paschali laudes* attributed to Wipo of Burgundy († *c.* 1040) with a non-rhymed text, uneven verses, introductory and concluding stanzas, represents a transitional stage; *Veni Sancte Spiritus* (variously attributed), *Lauda Sion* by St Thomas Aquinas, show rhymed texts and music typical of the school of Adam of St Victor, while the famous *Dies irae,* attributed to Thomas of Celano († *c.* 1250) is based on the rhymed trope added to the responsory in the absolutions after the Mass for the Dead. The

Council of Trent eliminated all the Sequences in the Mass except the four mentioned above, and *Stabat Mater* was only admitted in the seventeenth century.

THE LITURGICAL DRAMA

The practice of troping led to what is known as "liturgical drama", which developed out of the Easter Mass trope, *Quem quaeritis?* the words of which, a brief dialogue between the angel and the Maries at the empty tomb, are derived from the accounts given by all the Evangelists except St John. There are a few sentences of dialogue in the Sequence, *Victimae paschali laudes,* sung in the same Mass, in which Mary's words could be taken by a solo voice, but without anything one could call dramatization: and the above trope, according to the rubrics given in some manuscripts, was also sung in dialogue before the Mass, the Introit *Resurrexi* following on immediately. This trope is first found in the tenth century both at St Gall and Limoges and very soon all over Europe, showing additions and variations on the original. About the middle of the tenth century the trope was moved to the end of the night office of Matins and placed just before the *Te Deum* with which that Office concludes; Lauds would then follow as the day dawned. We now find the clerics who sung the trope were directed to put on robes suited to their parts, and so the way lay open for a truly dramatic representation of the scene and so for liturgical drama.

This early state of *Quem quaeritis* as true drama is found about 980 in the famous Anglo-Saxon service book *The Winchester Troper,* and this together with a full account of a performance by Ethelwold, Bishop of Winchester, gives us a good idea of the proceedings. The Visit to the Sepulchre became very popular throughout Europe and went through various stages of greater elaboration up to the thirteenth century, showing the way to other Easter plays and to those associated with the Nativity and other biblical and legendary subjects. The great success of the twelfth-century *Play of Daniel* in an edition by Noah Greenberg, and first performed in New York in 1950,[6] showed how much invention and vitality went into these music dramas. Mr Greenberg took over the version of the play made "by the youth of Beauvais" in the thirteenth century (an improvement on the drama by Hilarius made in the previous century) and though instruments are only once mentioned in the rubrics there are further references in the Latin verse which amply justify the use he has made of the modern equivalents of the medieval instruments.

The music was drawn by the medieval arrangers from various sources, melodic "tags" from plainsong, antiphons, hymns, sequences and secular melodies: and in such a piece as the famous Lament of Daniel we must surely have evidence of original composition. When members of the congregation took part in the plays, which one could well call sacred operas, various abuses arose and the plays were moved from the sanctuary down to the porch and then into the market place, and so, at length, into the theatre. And so it was the Church that, starting with the little *Quem quaeritis* trope enabled the drama to be reborn after the virtual eclipse of knowledge of the classical drama in the Dark Ages.

The eminent French musicologist, Coussemaker, in his source book, *Drames liturgiques du Moyen Age* (1860), of the text and music of twenty-two plays from manuscripts dating from the eleventh to the fourteenth centuries, quotes an imaginative passage by Adolphe Didron which it may be useful to recall when one is visiting a great cathedral and trying to picture its life in medieval times. "The three or four thousand statues and figures which people the portals and

<hr>

[6] This production was brought to Westminster Abbey in 1961 with the same success. On liturgical drama see in this series, Robert Speaight, *The Christian Theatre*.

windows of the cathedral of Chartres must have descended from their niches and panes . . . at least once a year, to play their drama in the nave and the choir of the vast edifice. In other words, the same events . . . as were sculptured in statues and painted on glass were played, at different festivals of the year, by living persons."

MOZARABIC, AMBROSIAN AND SARUM CHANT

Of the four great liturgies of the West, Roman, Ambrosian, Gallican and Mozarabic, only the first is in universal use today. Charlemagne suppressed the Gallican rite and the chant survives only in a few pieces from the Mass and in pieces so loved by the people that they were incorporated into Gregorian chant. It is probable, on the other hand, that the manuscripts of Mozarabic, or Visigothic, chant

> have preserved for us the entire music of the old Church of Toledo but only about twenty-one melodies that can be read are authentic, the remainder are concealed in the neumatic notation incapable of showing intervals and so, as the scribes did not bother to transcribe the melodies into staff notation, when the cathedral and parishes of Toledo were allowed to keep their own chant and when means were at hand to do so, the key to unlock this treasure chest is lost. [This is all the more exasperating as] the Spanish liturgy of the sixth and seventh centuries enshrines elements of the highest antiquity . . . the oldest Latin version of the Scriptures preserved comes from Spain, to which it had passed in the time of St Cyprian (third century) or even of Tertullian (second century) . . . (so) does the oldest liturgical Latin hymn with a refrain (given with its music in the Visigothic hymnal of the ninth or tenth century).

Peter Wagner thought that the Mozarabic *Pater Noster* might very well date from the fourth century.[7]

[7] *New Oxford History of Music*, Vol. II, "Latin Chant before St Gregory", p. 82, by Mgr Higini Anglès.

The situation is much more favourable in regard to the Ambrosian chant which with its rite won the battle for survival in the cathedral and diocese of Milan and which is contained in manuscripts in staff notation. The earliest of the manuscripts date back no further than the twelfth century, when the repertory of chant reached its fullest development, but many of its elements are ancient in origin. There are three distinct layers: the original are derived from the synagogue and early Eastern liturgies together with indigenous and popular strains, later Byzantine influences, and large Gregorian infiltrations. The Ambrosian chant shows a noticeable preference for small intervals, and is quite free of the modal system; it eschews word-painting and has a marked oriental flavour in the long florid passages called in the manuscripts *melodiae* or *tractus*. The repertoire is not large. Thus there are only a few chants for the Ordinary of the Mass, these being grouped in the original way, according to category, *Kyrie eleison* is not sung as a separate chant but at the end of the *Gloria*, and without *Christe eleison*. *Agnus Dei* is not sung except in the Requiem Mass. A notable feature of the Alleluias is that instead of, as in the Roman rite, being repeated, after the verse, as at the start they are greatly extended. They bear witness to Eastern ways of improvisation and also to the fusion of oriental and Franco-German forms. These are then among the most elaborate Ambrosian chants: the simpler ones, often with refrains, are very melodious.

Fr Rembrandt Weakland, an authority on this chant, writes: "One must accept Ambrosian chant for its own aesthetic and artistic musical expression. Our ears must become more accustomed to its roughness, its musical caprices, its sudden changes, and its peculiar exuberance. Perhaps our concept of medieval music has become too refined and too 'classical' so that we miss the charm in the freeness and fantasy of the Ambrosian chant."

A few words should now be said about the chants of the Sarum (Salisbury) Rite.

The Sarum rite is a "local medieval modification of the Roman rite in use at the cathedral Church of Salisbury". It was in use in nearly the whole of England, Wales and Ireland by 1427 and in 1543 the Canterbury Convocation imposed the Sarum Breviary on the whole province. Some of its chants are in use in the Anglican Church, with English words: and about forty of them with Latin texts—hymns and short pieces suitable for singing at Benediction—can be found in the manual *Laudate Dominum* compiled chiefly from English manuscripts. This little book should be better known.[8]

Salisbury was renowned for its music, as we can learn from Bishop Giles of Bridport who began his statute of 1256 with these words:

> The church of Salisbury shines as the sun in its orb among the churches of the whole world in its divine service and those who minister in it, and by spreading its rays everywhere makes up for the defects of others. Therefore, lest through our neglect its splendour should be diminished by the unworthiness of its ministers, we ordain that hereafter none shall be presented to the office of vicar in this church unless he has a good and musical voice and skill in plainsong, besides the merits of character required in such ministers.

It is sad to relate that not long after the dean and chapter of Salisbury had to rebuke the vicars choral for "disorderly gestures, movements, and leaping, signs of a levity of mind inconsistent with their dignity" and for "their perpetual restlessness in choir, running hither and thither, going out and returning without any obvious reason". But this was an occupational ailment of "choirs and places where they sing", recurring from time to time and in this case, no doubt, due to Salisbury's high reputation going to their heads.

[8] *Song-Schools in the Middle Ages* by A. Hamilton Thompson, S.P.C.K., London, 1942.

THE GÉLINEAU PSALMODY

The long neglect of the congregational singing of psalms in the Roman Church, persisting even after the Gregorian revival in the nineteenth century, has been repaired with notable success in France and Great Britain with the introduction of what has become known as the Gélineau Psalmody.

Fr Joseph Gélineau, S.J., was inspired to bring about a new way of singing the psalms when he read the French translation of the Psalter made from the Hebrew by the compilers of the *Bible de Jérusalem*. It was the aim of those at work on this translation to reproduce, as faithfully as possible, as Dom Gregory Murray wrote,[9] "not only the simple, direct flavour of the original Hebrew, but also its very rhythm", a rhythm which Dom Murray equates with the "sprung rhythm" in the poems of Gerard Manley Hopkins. The stanza as it stood in the Hebrew psalms had three to six lines, and not the artificial division of the Latin "verse" so familiar to us, and being restored as the unit revealed the true poetic structure of the psalms.

Fr Gélineau and his helpers, therefore, set themselves the task of devising means of putting music to the newly translated psalms of a simple enough nature to make it possible for all but the tone deaf to join in wholly or, at least, partially. There was no intention to displace such plainsong as congregations could attempt and these new psalm settings, using the vernacular, could not, of course, be introduced directly into the liturgy but, as we shall see, they could be sung during the people's Communion at Mass, at missions, baptisms, weddings, funerals or during night prayers before Benediction.

The rhythm of the stanzas is based on the regular recurrence of accented syllables, which in the texts in the Gélineau music books are shown in heavy black type. The number of

[9] In the *Downside Review*, Vol. 74, pp. 95 ff.

accents, or stresses, is fixed for each stanza but the number of unstressed syllables is, of course, variable. One example will suffice to show the system followed:

> Out of the *depths* I cry to you O *Lord*,
> *Lord*, hear my voice!
> O *let* your *ears* be attentive
> To the *voice* of my *pleading*.   (Psalm 129)

White notes are used for accented syllables, black ones for unaccented ones. There is always an introductory beat to accommodate the variable number of syllables occurring before the first accent, but the second beat will occur punctually on the first accent. Father Gélineau suggests a metronome setting between 48 and 72, giving a slow enough basic tempo to provide for clear enunciation of the words.

The Gélineau melodies must not be thought of as psalm tones, with intonation, reciting note, mediant and final cadences as in Gregorian psalmody, but as free melodies to be performed as near as possible to the old rule "sing as you speak", that is, simply and naturally. The music, we are told, was inspired in a wide sense by the old liturgical music of various rites, Ambrosian, Armenian, Roman and also by folk-songs; it keeps strictly to the modalism of the Gregorian tradition. It follows that the antiphons provided have the same modal relation to the psalms as in the Latin rite, but the music of the antiphons has its own rhythmic structure —they are given time signatures—and must be rendered to the same regular beat as the psalm to which they are attached. In some cases alternative antiphons are given, but antiphons can be entirely dispensed with. Variety of treatment is one of the most valuable features of the Gélineau psalmody and whichever way is chosen it will be in line with the ancient practice of the Church. Thus the "direct" method—the oldest of all—may be used in which a soloist sings the entire psalm, the people listening and *understanding* (for it is in the vernacular): or the people themselves can sing the psalm through, or they can repeat the antiphon—after it has been "patterned" by the singers—after each verse, thus singing responsorially, and so forth.

Without waiting for the completion of the *Bible de Jérusalem* Psalter, Fr Gélineau issued his *Vingt-quatre Psaumes et un Cantique* in 1953. It rapidly sold 200,000 copies and the first long-playing gramophone record must now have long surpassed the 30,000 copies it sold with almost equal rapidity. Further volumes and recordings have followed and the success of the movement must have surpassed Fr Gélineau's wildest imaginings. The Gélineau psalms are in use in churches, seminaries, colleges and can, of course, be used by any Christian denomination: and are being so used.

The movement did not long go unnoticed in England and Fr Gélineau gladly acceded to a request from the enterprising Ladies of the Grail, a lay community, that they might be allowed to issue an English edition of his first book. This task was ably carried out and, as Fr Gélineau had predicted, the Hebrew accentual system proved to be more suited to English than to French. He wisely and perceptively suggested that new antiphons should be composed for the English edition, many of his own having, he considered, too French a flavour. The new antiphons were composed by Fr Clifford Howell, S.J., and Dom Gregory Murray and in the later book also by Dom Lawrence Bévenot, Fr Wilfrid Trotman, and others.

The Grail also published accompaniments, and vocal harmonizations, for some of the psalms, and have issued to date two ten-inch long-playing discs showing the different ways in which the psalms can be sung.

There is one danger in this "new" way of singing the psalms, which has been also very successful in Great Britain, and that is that the people may, unless encouraged and well directed, content themselves with singing the antiphons, particularly the very tuneful ones, as they may legitimately do occasionally, leaving choirs to sing the psalms, often in four parts, or with hummed harmonies to the voice of a soloist, thus robbing the whole idea of its simplicity and spontaneity.

It is indeed thrilling to hear a vast congregation, as the writer once did in Chartres Cathedral, sing with one accord the refrain (antiphon) to Psalm 135, *Car éternel est son amour,* during the distribution of Holy Communion, but it was the cathedral choir that sang the psalm, not the congregation.

This writer feels that efforts should continue to be made to teach people to sing, in Gregorian chant, the psalms and canticle at Vespers and both psalms, canticle, hymn, and antiphons (only one for the psalm group) at Compline. It is absurd to say this is too ambitious a project since the short psalm *Laudate Dominus omnes gentes* is easily accomplished at Benediction by the ordinary mixed congregation and the boys of the Catholic public schools sing the psalms at Vespers with heartening brio. If ever we are granted a vernacular Vespers and Compline then the Gélineau method would come liturgically into its own: but nothing should ever be allowed to drive the ancient song of the Church out of the sanctuary. No one would agree about that more heartily than Fr Gélineau.

BYZANTINE CHANT

Byzantine chant, often mentioned in this book, seems—like the rite to which it is attached—very remote to us and opportunities for hearing it are all too infrequent. Whereas a fairly large repertoire of Gregorian and Ambrosian chants is now available on disc there are, at present, only three short examples of Byzantine chant to be had, and these not very convincingly sung by an English choir. It is to be hoped that this very unsatisfactory state of affairs may be remedied. We are well informed about the Eastern liturgies—two books in this series are devoted to it—and Dr Egon Wellesz, in addition to his fine book on *A History of Byzantine Music and Hymnography* (republished in 1961 in an enlarged edition), has edited an admirably chosen series of chants, with a preface and English translations of the texts, in the *Anthology of Music*, a collection of complete musical examples illustrating the history of music, edited by Karl Gustav Fellerer: but one does want to hear the music sung. Dr Wellesz writes:

> The circumstance that only manuscripts later than the twelfth century can be used to transcribe Byzantine melodies, as they are the earliest to give intervals definitely, should not be taken to mean that the melodies or versions are of this date. Comparative studies have shown that from the tenth century onward the chants in the heirmologic style, and the greater part of those in the sticheraric style, remained the same, and only varied in minimal detail in the course of three centuries. . . . It is, in the first place, the repertory of the Eastern Church, silenced for more than half a millennium, that is now revealed. But over and above this, our knowledge of the early stages of Western liturgical chant is widened through the recovery of the melodies of the Eastern Church: we stand, however, only at the beginning of these studies. Only when the greater part of the Eastern Church's melodic treasures are published shall we be able to draw full profit from the conclusions that have already been reached by comparative liturgiology.

Elsewhere Dr Wellesz makes the interesting point "that there is no period of the development of Byzantine chant which can be regarded as representing its purest state" as it was never looked on, as Gregorian chant was, as a more or less closed art after the eighth century, in spite of additions such as the majority of the chants of the Ordinary of the Mass. The Byzantine Church "from its earliest days encouraged the composition of hymns and did not object either to the introduction of new hymns or, from the thirteenth century onwards, to changes in the music by the introduction of ever-increasing embellishment".

CELTIC CHANT

The Celtic Church, as defined in the *Oxford Dictionary of the Christian Church*, is "the name generally applied to the Church which existed in the British Isles before the mission of St Augustine in 596–7 . . . a Church founded by the second or third century at latest by missions from Rome or Gaul". The coming of the Saxons in the second half of the fifth century more or less destroyed the Celtic Church and its culture in England, but Christian outposts in Cornwall, Wales, Scotland and Ireland survived although cut off from Rome and the Continent. It is not surprising that they developed great independence and resisted St Augustine of Canterbury's attempts to make them conform to Rome. Dom Louis Gougaud's admirable book *Christianity in Celtic Lands* gives a full and fascinating picture of the rise and development of Celtic Christianity, but in the section dealing with "Christian Arts" there is unfortunately little that he is able to tell us of the music in use in the monasteries and generally in the ritual of worship.

St Gildas (*c*. 500–70), monk and first British historian, speaks briefly of the "tuneful voices of Christ's servants, sweetly modulated, singing the praises of God" and of "the strains of ecclesiastical melody", but he gives no information as to what melodies were used.

The earliest reference to the use of the organ to accompany "sacred hymns", Dom Gougaud tells us, is found in the life of St Paul Aurelian, written by Wrmonoc in the ninth century. The Welsh historian Giraldus Cambrensis (1147–1223) describes the Irish music as having particular charm and its melodies as not "slow and harsh" as those of his native country but "quick and lively, albeit sweet and blithe in tone". He names the *cithara* (harp) as the chief instrument in use in Ireland, Scotland and Wales, and informs us that the bishops, abbots and saints of Ireland were accustomed to carry their harps (which differed in size, shape and number of strings) with them on their journeys, awaking pious delight by their playing in their listeners. We know, also, from other sources, that St Aldhelm, the patron saint of Dorset, danced and sang his own melodies in the streets of Sherborne for the joy of the Gospel.

Dom Gougaud considers that there is no evidence at all to suggest that Irish monks took an important part—or even any part—in the development of Gregorian chant. This theory grew out of the presence of the Irish monk Moengal († 869) who settled at St Gall and who was said by Ekkehard to be *maxime autem ad musicam*. W. H. Grattan Flood (1859–1928), Irish organist and musical scholar, wrote copiously on this subject, holding that Tuotillo, who died at St Gall in the same year as his friend Notker and wrote a number of tropes, was also an Irishman; but this richly gifted man, skilled in the plastic arts as well as music, was more probably a Swabian. The most that can be said in the present state of our knowledge is that there may be Celtic strains in Notker's music due to Moengal. One must deeply regret that our information about the plainsong of the Celtic Church is so meagre.

We have ample evidence of the beauty of their prayers and blessings, collections of which have notably been made by Alexander Carmichael; and long before St Francis came into the world, Celtic Christianity showed a great love of nature and of country, an intimate friendship with animals as well as angels, and a passion for spirituality. H. J. Massingham in his book *The Tree of Life* has given a vivid picture of the hard and austere life some of these monks must have lived, evidence of which can still be seen at the places here described.

The monastic cells of Skellig Michael, the lump of crag off the coast of Kerry, were built on a platform 600 feet above the sea—five small beehive huts and two minute oratories, dry-walled and fenced within a wall whose outer face was flush with the precipice that walls the sea . . . here the brethren lived like a herd of goats. The wildest isles round the wild Irish coast, the Blaskets, Inishmurray, the Arans, Clare and others were alike populated by these auk-men, and the sound of their plainsong must have often accompanied the hoarse primordial roar of the massed guillemots, itself corresponding to the more measured beat of the breakers and of the booming of the wind. In that primal scene the ear would often have caught a graded series of variations upon a single theme of elemental majesty, the tumult of the wind and sea translated into the growling thunder of the white-breasted bird-ranks, and that in its turn transfigured into the harmonious *Magnificat* of the monkish antiphony. For these sainted sea-dogs were a bardic company. I have stroked an eider-duck on its pillow-nest among the thrift in the little sea-garden of St Cuthbert's Monastery on the Faeroes—and its downiest home among the elements—and in the act repeated what St Cuthbert doubtless did every summer day as due part of his Matins.

It has been worth while to reproduce this imaginative passage in order to draw attention to the neglected subject of the Celtic Church. Perhaps we can catch an echo of their extra-liturgical music in some such exquisite melody as "The Christ-Child Lullaby" collected by Mrs Marjorie Kennedy Fraser in the first volume of *Songs of the Hebrides*.

CHAPTER III

THE INTRODUCTION AND DEVELOPMENT OF POLYPHONY UP TO THE FOURTEENTH CENTURY

Guido of Arezzo (*c.* 995–1050), the great theorist to whom we owe the invention of solmization (tonic sol-fa), speaks in one of his treatises of things which be easily explained by word of mouth though difficult to write about; and any writer on the introduction of polyphony (music in two parts or more) will ruefully applaud the sentiment. The writings of the theorists in the ninth century are, as usual, far from clear and musicologists of our time are not agreed as to how polyphony came into the Church. The organ was introduced into France from Constantinople in the latter half of the eighth century but one cannot believe that this noisy instrument, played by "two or three brethren of concordant spirit", pounding with all their strength on the "slides" (keys), can have suggested anything but a desire to get as far away from it as possible! This indeed was said of the monster tenth-century organ at Winchester: "Everyone stops with his hands his gaping ears, being in no wise able to draw near and hear the sound." Even on a much smaller instrument the quality of tone cannot have been agreeable, but it is just possible that the sounding of two notes simultaneously may have been suggestive. The curious change of pitch in Alleluia Sequences wherein a phrase may be repeated a fifth higher (as, for example, in *Dies irae*), making what is awkward for baritones easy for tenors, may have led to a simultaneous performance in both pitches at once; or the simple kind of polyphony, without real harmonic implications (known to the Greeks and in the East, and found among primitive races and in folk music), may have exerted an irresistible influence on a conservative Church. Whatever impulse brought it about the earliest form of polyphony in the Church called *organum* (derived probably from the Latin verb *organare*, to organize) was not the beginning of harmony so much as the enrichment of the single melodic line. Thus, from a famous tenth-century treatise *Musica Enchiriadis* we discover that there were four types of *organum*, (1) plainsong on the top line, doubled below at the fifth, (2) the plainsong also doubled at the octave below with the "organizing voice" doubled an octave above, resulting in four-part writing, (3) four parts in parallel fourths, (4) two parts, but with the lower part—below the plainsong—remaining stationary at certain points. The result of doubling, except in (4), could hardly be called harmony: but one can imagine it was an exciting experience for the singers, and it can sound impressive to our ears today. From an account of the dedication of Romsey Abbey, in 991, we learn that "while the Decani side of the choir sang a melodious strain with excellent voices, the Cantoris side laboured at *organum* parts in joyful songs of praise". One side, therefore, sung the unadorned plainsong, the other "organized" it.

The next innovation was to introduce contrary motion: and this we find in the collection of 164 two-part *organa* known as the Winchester Troper, which dates from the early part of the eleventh century. In this manuscript the organal part is placed *above* the plainsong and so foreshadows the firm bass part which is the essence of classical harmony. Unfortunately, the music of the Winchester Troper is in neumatic not staff notation and so the interpretation of this manuscript remains conjectural; but another eleventh-century manuscript, using alphabetical notation, can be read and shows the variety of intervals used: octaves, unisons, fourths, fifths, but only one sixth and three major thirds.[1]

England made what appears to be a unique contribution in the shape of parallel *organum* in thirds, later to be called *gymel*, or twin-song, a style that might well be derived from popular music and allied to the kind of singing "one murmuring in the bass, the other warbling in the acute or treble", that Gerald de Barri (1147–1220) noted "in the Northern district of Britain beyond the Humber and on the borders of Yorkshire", together with singing in more than two parts in Wales. But his account, in *Descriptio Cambriae*, is regarded by musicologists as that of an imprecise amateur. The Church, which had only tolerated troping, was likely to keep a wary eye on polyphony, and we find that strict instructions were given as to which sections of Mass and Office polyphony could be applied. In line with the general and natural custom in plainsong the more important the feast, the greater the amount of elaboration allowed.

The nature of psalmody dictated that only antiphons should be given "organized" setting: in hymns and Sequences only even-numbered verses were set, a practice which we meet with up to the first half of the seventeenth century; solo sections in responsorial chants were set, chorus sections being left in plainsong.

The monastery of Cluny, founded in 910 by William the Pious, Duke of Aquitaine, became under St Odo, its abbot from 927, a great spiritual, liturgical and musical centre whose influence was widespread. Today Dijon Cathedral,

[1] *Lucca MS.* 603.

formerly the Cluniac monastery of St Bénigne, keeps the high standard of its predecessors. It does not impose such strict discipline on the choirboys who in earlier days if they committed any fault in the psalmody or other singing, "either by sleeping or such like transgressions were without delay stripped of frock and cowl, beaten in their shirt only with pliant and smooth osier rods provided for that special purpose". When one considers the enormous amount of music the boys had to learn by heart and the long services they had to attend, it cannot have been easy to avoid either faults or somnolence.

The so-called free organum of the eleventh century, as contrasted with parallel organum, shows note against note writing in contrary motion and the principle of alternation between soloists, for the polyphonic sections, and chorus for the plainsong already mentioned. In the following century a type of organum, known as melismatic organum, was cultivated at the Abbey of St Martial, Limoges, and St James' Compostela (now Santiago, Spanish for St James), a great pilgrimage centre. The plainsong, in the lower part, is now wholly robbed of its natural rhythm and put into notes of indeterminate length above which the "organal" voice moves in florid phrases; but with, here and there, the two parts coming together in the previous note against note type of writing.

Gregorian chant remained, of course, a liturgical necessity and the norm of church music, but it became a mine of musical themes, the *canti fermi* or fixed songs, upon the basis of which composers exercised their skill in polyphonic writing. There were many technical problems to be solved of which the most difficult was the notating of exact time values to enable several voices to sing together in a disciplined way. In free and melismatic organum there would have been some understanding, intuitive or settled, as to when the lower and sustained note part would move, and it would be governed by points of consonance, the pillars, so to speak, of the architecture irregularly placed.

MEASURED MUSIC

Whereas Gregorian chant finds its architectural counterpart in the churches of the Romanesque period, the measured music we have now to deal with is allied to the cathedrals of the Gothic period, those "mounting prayers in stone and glass that from about 1180 to 1250 were offered by the religious fervour of Germany, England, Spain and—first and foremost—France" with the cathedral of Notre-Dame de Paris as its great musical centre, and its finest achievement, the glorious cathedral of Notre-Dame de Chartres.

In a moving passage about Notre-Dame, Paris, William Waite writes:

> In the twelfth and thirteenth centuries (it) had become the focal point of intellectual Europe and its stones still stand as testimony of the visions and aspirations of this age. Its portals tell with their sculptural friezes of a hierarchic world order in which every being has its place; its symmetrical façade and ordered interior space portray a world where all is regulated by consonance and proportion. Indeed the Cathedral of Notre-Dame, like other masterpieces of Gothic architecture erected in this same period, still sings the silent hymn of the men who created it, a paean of praise to a universe framed in musical proportions and linked from extremity to extremity by the harmonizing force of musical numbers. But while Notre-Dame even today bears mute witness to the medieval conception of a musical cosmos, the music, which once echoed from its walls . . . has been forgotten.[2]

This is not wholly true. Amédée Gastoué revived some of the works of Perotinus at the Sainte-Chapelle in 1914 during a Congress of the International Society of Music and thirteen

[2] Sleeve note of gramophone record *Notre Dame Organa: Leoninus and Perotinus Magister, Expérience Anonymes*, New York, 1957.

years later Dr Rudolph Ficker followed his example, using the choir of the Vienna Hofburg, during the Beethoven Centenary commemorations. On both occasions many who had considered the music to be only of historical interest were amazed at its beauty. "This was a revelation, a flash of beauty, like the windows of Chartres or of Bourges, suddenly illuminated by the sun." Ficker's reconstructions of masters of the Notre-Dame school were also performed by the *Schola Cantorum* in New York. The two outstanding masters of the Notre-Dame school were Léonin and Pérotin, and by a fortunate chance an English monk from Bury St Edmunds took copious notes on a lecture course in music which he attended at the Sorbonne and thus illuminated for future scholars this period of musical history. He tells us that Léonin was the best composer of organum. "He wrote the Great Book of organa, for Mass and Office, to enlarge the divine service. The book was used until the time of the great Pérotin, who shortened it and rewrote many sections in a better way. Pérotin was the best composer of discant—he was better than Léonin—he wrote the best four-part organa . . . with the most ample embellishments of harmonic art."

Léonin, between *c*. 1150 and 1175, composed a cycle of pieces in two parts for all the responsorial chants of Mass, Vespers and Matins on major feasts. His organa resembled the melismatic type mentioned above, that is, the plainsong, in long sustained notes, is the "tenor" or holding-part, above which notes of varying length were used in varying rhythmic patterns.

In his setting of the Gradual *Haec dies*, for example, there are just over 100 notes, short and long—crotchets, quavers and occasionally semiquavers in our terminology—to the eighteen sustained notes in the tenor. The drone-like tenor part and the arabesques in the upper part together produce a faintly oriental effect. There are sections in this Gradual reserved to the soloists called *clausula*, a word meaning cadence, but here used for strict contrapuntal writing in *both* parts, both using one word (even on occasion one syllable of a word) of the text.

Léonin's *clausula* lengthened the Gradual unduly and it was for those sections that Pérotin (perhaps his pupil) provided substitutes. He seems to have been the first to use three or four parts; the lower one may well have been played on an instrument.

Besides the forms of organum there was the *conductus* sung at moments in the Mass when one of the ministers—for example a deacon—was led or "conducted" to his position for intoning the Gospel. The Gradual in *conductus* style would use no plainsong tenor but a newly composed melody or one borrowed from a non-liturgical source: all the parts would partake of the same rhythm and be simple in style. There is a large collection of such processional pieces, and of others, some monophonic, not meant for liturgical use. One of these latter, *Alleluia psallat*, in three parts, became very popular and remains so today. It dances along free from any shackles and with a gaiety that belongs to the open air. It is true that the lowest part quotes a plainsong Alleluia just near the end, but the provenance of this charming piece is the village green rather than the cloister.

THE MOTET

The motet is another form to be considered here. It developed out of the *clausula* as the Sequence developed out of the Alleluia—that is, words were added to it. What emerged was a three-part structure in which the lowest part, usually a plainsong theme, was sung or more probably played on an instrument—a viol or the organ. It differed wholly from the kind of motet familiar to us today in the works of, let us say, Josquin, Palestrina or Byrd, a form in which all the parts are not independent but in which one part imitates the other.

In the thirteenth-century motet the omission of one of the parts would still leave the other two sounding well. It follows that there could be no imitative writing. These motets, usually in three parts, were often polytextual—and sometimes even polylingual. And so *triplum* (treble) and *motetus* parts might each have their own texts in honour of Our Lady. Thus, *O Maria Virgo Davidica* and *Ave maris stella*, with the tenor drawing its theme from a related plainsong source. Theologically it was satisfying to have one part made complementary to another in this way even if one could not hear both texts when the motet was sung, but it laid itself open to abuse. Secular Latin and French texts began to appear not only in purely secular pieces inspired by the liturgical motet but in that type of motet itself: and it also was made the vehicle of absolutely contradictory texts. Thus some witty, or malicious, person composed a motet in which the text of the middle part spoke of "the pious priests' work shining like stars of the firmament" but the upper part reviled the priests as "hypocritical, malicious, drunken, lecherous . . . tormentors of the Church", while the plainsong tenor comes from the verse of the Alleluia in the octave of the Ascension, "I will not leave you orphans, I will come to you", our Lord's parting words. It is easy enough to read the composer's intentions but difficult to believe such motets were ever sung complete in church. The upper part would be discreetly omitted and perhaps sung outside the church by some rebellious or ribald faction!

The art of polyphony had found, in general, a warm welcome amongst musicians and other people capable of appreciating it, but not invariably among learned ecclesiastics and scholars. Having no prophetic vision of the glories still to come they saw in the existing polyphony used in church a dangerous intrusion of the secular spirit and no doubt found it compared very unfavourably with the spiritual and ordered beauty of Gregorian chant. One can hardly blame these conservatives when a Latin liturgical text was married to a French love-song in one and the same motet, or some polemic text such as the one quoted above was discovered. John of Salisbury (*c.* 1115–80), medieval philosopher, was among those who had raised objections to this "disorganized" music in its best days, and deplored the pleasure taken by the singers in "the manifold *cantilenae*": we, for our part, marvel at the skill these musicians must have possessed. When John of Salisbury goes so far as to say that such music "defiled the service of religion" he anticipated the Avignon pope, John XXII, who, in 1324, forbade all but the simplest kind of harmonization of liturgical chant—a return almost to early organum—and castigated singers who "truncate the melodies with hockets,[3] deprave them with discants, and even trope the upper parts with secular songs". However, as we know from the immediate fate of the *Motu proprio* of Pius X it takes more than a papal decree to stop abuses in music. This kind died a natural death, hastened by the increasing importance of secular music itself in the fourteenth century which claimed composers' attention. But in spite of the abuses music would be the poorer without the many lovely Marian motets, with complementary texts, which testify to the ever growing devotion to the Mother of God.

The organa, *clausula* and motet had been subjected to the shackles of modal rhythms, that is to a set of rhythmic patterns in a ternary metre: but in the second half of the thirteenth century Pierre de la Croix of Amiens, another composer of the Notre-Dame School, had freed the upper parts of his motets from these rhythmic modes and given the music greater melodic and rhythmic independence. This emancipation led, by slow degrees, to the abandonment of the modal rhythms and the development out of them of the isorhythmic motet, the form that, as we shall see, prevailed in the fourteenth century. This century was given the title of *Ars Nova*

---

[3] A kind of musical hiccough, "one part resting (for a beat) while the other sings".

in a treatise by Philip de Vitry (*c.* 1291–1361) who wished to contrast it with the *Ars Antiqua* of the preceding century. Amid wars, peasant rebellions, the plague of the Black Death and general moral corruption, amid every sign of the collapse of the medieval order, but with the repeated demands of a clear-sighted minority for a reformation of Church and society, music comes into this transitional period of the *Ars Nova*, with France as its centre. Its main achievements were in the secular field. A new lyricism flowers, duple metre is recognized and the growing use of chromatic notes (*musica ficta*) points the church modes along the long road to the modern major–minor tonality of our time.

Pope John had not forbidden in polyphonic church music "certain consonances which gave a savour to the melody, such as the octave, the fifth and fourth which may be sung above the simple ecclesiastical melody in such a way that the integrity of the chant itself remains intact and nothing in the authoritative music changed". Taken literally, as has been hinted above, this could only mean simple organum, but this ruling, as severe as any proposed at the Council of Trent, proved far too limiting, and in France—and so within range of the pope at Avignon—a device emerged by which the singing of the lower parts of chords (which look like simple organum) an octave above turned them into chords of the sixth. This *faulx bourdon*, or false bass, was not however restricted to such chords, and from it there begins a feeling for successions of chords, regarded vertically, instead of chords resulting from melodies regarded horizontally.

The greatest name in the church music of the *Ars Nova* period is that of Guillaume de Machaut (*c.* 1300–77), priest, poet, composer, lover of hunting and master of the isorhythmic motet. This technique, as such, like much serialism today, is for the eye rather than the ear and the great skill in working it out is at the expense of freely flowing melody. Isorhythm has been briefly defined as variations on a rhythmic skeleton that remains unchanged throughout. To enlarge on this: a melody is stretched on a Procrustean bed of a predetermined rhythmic pattern; if it is too long for the rhythmic pattern it continues when the rhythmic pattern begins again; if it is too short it continues before the repeat of the rhythmic pattern, the result being rhythmic variety. One or more of the parts in a motet were subjected to this technique.

Machaut's only setting of the Mass, the *Messe de Notre Dame*, is probably the earliest complete polyphonic setting of the Ordinary by one composer, for the *Messe de Tournai* is a collection of movements by a number of composers. (It is worth remembering that a number of plainsong settings of parts of the Ordinary were still appearing in this century.) The Tournai Mass is simple compared to Machaut's rhythmically elaborate and harmonically adventurous setting. He uses isorhythmic technique and plainsong tenors in the *Kyrie, Sanctus, Agnus Dei* and *Ite, missa est:* but the longer texts of the *Gloria* and *Credo* are freely composed. The Mass achieves a unity not only by the use of plainsong but also of a short motive, heard on instruments as well as voices (for the Mass is instrumentally accompanied) which comes into each section. Machaut leaves the initial phrases of *Gloria* and *Credo* to be intoned by the celebrant, and sets the words *Jesu Christe* in the *Gloria* and *ex Maria Virgine* in the *Credo* to notes of longer value so as to emphasize their solemnity. Harmonically the music is remarkable—the sudden acute dissonance at *crucifixus* still arrests the ear—but rhythmically it is too complex for the ear to follow and the use of "hocketting" in the *Benedictus* will sound strange to ears unacquainted with the period.

Isorhythmic technique was not favoured in Italy, although "the motet was cultivated to a degree which is not even remotely indicated by the manuscripts".

A bas-relief in the Church of San Lorenzo, Florence, shows Francesco Landini, who lost his sight in early childhood, playing on a little portative organ with two angel musicians hovering about his head. Though this famous organist, whose playing was the admiration of Florence, composed some exquisite secular music the angels failed, apparently, to inspire him to compose church music unless some *Kyrie* and *Gloria* pieces for keyboard designed to alternate with each section of the sung plainsong are by him.

LAUDE SPIRITUALI

Florence was the centre of musical life in the fourteenth century, Rome was a dead city, with the popes at Avignon, and would not revive until their return the following century: but all over Italy, as in France, secular music predominated and excelled. We may, however, turn aside for a moment to the lovely music of the *Laude* which was purely religious in origin.

Lauda was a name used to describe a song performed by societies of lay singers in the eleventh and twelfth centuries and these *Laude* were really sacred songs in the vernacular, based on popular melodies, which took the place of the Latin liturgical hymns no longer intelligible to the people.

The Umbrian *Laude* were written in the dialects of the shepherd and labourers and dealt, as does St Francis of Assisi's glorious *Canticle of the Sun,* with "the elemental and enduring things that are the essential background and frequent inspiration of Italian folk-songs". The Tuscan *Laude* were chiefly lyrical: but those of Umbria soon took on dramatic shape and it is from them that the Italian drama of the Middle Ages derives its origin. The most famous of the Franciscan poets, Jacopone da Todi (1228–1306), to whom *Stabat Mater* is doubtfully attributed, went about the towns of Umbria singing in the market place songs drawn from "the inexhaustible vein of grief and repentance". The miseries of the previous century, which threw the people into a state of apathy and despair, were interpreted by the Franciscans as signs of divine displeasure and they encouraged the formation of companies of flagellants to do penance for the sins of an uncaring, pleasure-ridden world. They wended their way through the streets scourging themselves, singing the while the kind of hymns that became known as *Laude spirituali*. The movement spread rapidly and widely and after the original impulse died away the confraternities of singers remained in being. By the sixteenth century the *Laude* were no longer simple unison melodies sung out of doors but songs in three or four parts sung in churches and houses. When St Philip of Neri founded his Congregation of the Oratory in Rome he made much use of the form and Giovanni Animuccia, the papal chapel-master and contemporary of Palestrina, composed, as many others did, *Laude spirituali* for use in the Oratory.

CHAPTER IV

ENGLISH CHURCH MUSIC TO THE SIXTEENTH CENTURY

Divisions of history, we are warned by historians, are arbitrary and misleading: and indeed it would be obviously absurd to assert that the Middle Ages ended and the Renaissance began on this or that date. In regard to music the first half or so of the fifteenth century is a period of consolidation of the "Gothic" techniques handed down by the previous century and of transition into the Renaissance. It is, for the student of musical history, a most interesting and fruitful century both abroad and at home.

English composers emerge from anonymity and come fully into the light in the famous manuscript known as the Old Hall from its presence since 1893 in the Library of St Edmund's College, Old Hall, Ware. It consists of 140 folios of music for the Ordinary of the Mass (and in its original state some antiphons and motets) by composers of the Chapel Royal. Latest research holds that though the manuscript originated in the reign of Henry V (1413–22) the oldest and largest part of it was written in the reign of Henry IV (1399–1413). The long list of composers, which includes some sturdy English names such as Dammett, Sturgeon, Pycard and Swynford, has in the Mass settings a *Gloria* and *Sanctus* variously attributed in the past to Henry IV, V and VI; but it is now held to be almost certainly by Henry IV.

> The first layer contains pieces in "English descant" and more elaborate compositions which show decided continental influence. . . . The second layer, added by two scribes, contains music by composers who appear in the "chapel" in the first year of Henry V, and further compositions by two of the first group . . . (it may be) dated between 1413–32. . . . The final addition of pieces by Dunstable and Forest may possibly have been made at the time of the chapel's visit to France in 1430–1.[1]

The richness of this collection throws into high relief the paucity of English manuscripts that have come down to us from the fourteenth century. Not one of them has survived complete: and those we have are preserved on leaves, or groups of leaves, some of which have been used as binding material—with nearly as much damage as to Haydn's manuscripts used by his shrewish wife to line her baking tins!

There are, however, enough clues to show the trends in composition fully exposed in the Old Hall manuscript. To describe these would involve an excursion into technical details outside the scope of this small book and it will be more profitable to say something about the two greatest composers found in the manuscript. These are John Dunstable who was born some time towards the end of the fourteenth century and died in 1453 and Leonel Power, of whom we only know that he died at Canterbury in 1445. Dunstable, who was described by the Abbot of St Albans as "astronomer, musician, mathematician and what not", was buried at St Stephen's Walbrook. His fame radiated out beyond his own country and drew from Johannes Tinctoris, the Flemish theoretician and choirmaster at the court of Ferdinand of Aragon in Naples, the tribute that music "in our time took

[1] Frank Harrison, *Music in Medieval Britain*, pp. 221–2.

such a wonderful flight because it seems to be a new art which
originated with the English under the leadership of Dunstable"; while Martin le Franc, in a poem called *Le Champion des Dames*, written about 1440, testifies to the influence
Dunstable had on his Burgundian contemporaries Dufay and
Binchois:

> The English guise they wear with grace:
> They follow Dunstable aright,
> And thereby have they learned apace
> To make their music gay and bright.

The presence of manuscripts of Dunstable's compositions
in so many places on the Continent and particularly in Italy
—whereas there are so few in England—shows that he may
have spent much of his time abroad. The melodic and harmonic charm of his music is due in part to the characteristically English use of thirds and sixths and love of sonority of
sound, and in part to Italian influence. In his church music
Dunstable makes a welcome return to liturgical ideals, ex-
cluding secular texts in his motets, but sometimes replacing
the traditional borrowed plainsong melody with a freely composed part.

Dunstable's settings of *Quam pulchra es* (text from the
Song of Songs) for solo voice and two instruments and *Sancta
Maria*, for three voices, are two of his loveliest motets in
freely composed style. The melody and rhythm of the first
of these have a fresh simplicity about them that is most
appealing and the lucid harmony shows the English love of
chords of the third and sixth all through. *Sancta Maria* is
more elaborate and has a more closely woven texture. The
middle and lower voices alone, and upper and middle voices
alone, form duet sections of contrast to the use of the three
voices together. This points to the extensive use of independent duet sections in Mass and motet polyphony from the
fifteenth to the end of the sixteenth century.

An independent section of the kind appears in Power's

Anima mea liquefacta est, a solo motet with two-part instrumental accompaniment, and sections in both of purely instrumental writing. Both Dunstable and Power are given to writing of great rhythmic complexity. A famous example is Dunstable's four-part motet *Veni sancte Spiritus* in which he manages to permeate the isorhythmic technique—described above (pp. 68–9)—with characteristically euphonious harmony. The composer, oddly enough, sets the words of the Sequence *Veni sancte Spiritus* in the treble part, to the melody of the hymn *Veni Creator Spiritus,* freely treated after the first nine bars, and employs this melody in the tenor part to some of its words; while the alto's words are a trope of *Veni sancte Spiritus* and the contra-tenor has the original text. Polytextuality, which looked to the past, is a feature of his other thirteen isorhythmic motets.

To Power is ascribed the earliest cyclic Mass in complete form that has come down to us; that is to say, the movements of the Mass are unified by the use in each one of a plainsong theme, in this case the plainsong of the Marian antiphon *Alma Redemptoris Mater,* which gives the Mass its title. Power also anticipated the practice of reducing the voices in the sections of the *Sanctus* beginning *Pleni sunt coeli* and *Benedictus qui venit* which was to become standard for the next century and a half.

No wholly satisfactory reasons have been given for the English habit of rarely composing a polyphonic *Kyrie*—it was usually sung in plain chant to a troped text and in modern times music from the *Agnus Dei* is used to supply a polyphonic setting for it—and of omitting a large section of *Credo,* from after *Cujus regni non erit finis* to *Et vitam venturi saeculi* or even to *Amen.* This latter habit persisted into the reign of Henry VIII. The solution may be that some of the Henrician Masses were already very long, but the additional time required for the omitted clauses (which would, of course, have been said by the celebrant) would not have made much difference. Dunstable and others, using thirteenth-century motet technique, set some clauses simultaneously—for example, *et resurrexit, et ascendit*—and this practice is found as late as the nineteenth century in, for example, Cherubini's D minor Requiem Mass for three male voices.

It is possible that Dunstable's motet *Veni sancte Spiritus* and his *Credo* and *Sanctus*, the two existing movements of a perhaps complete polyphonic Ordinary of the Mass based on the plainsong *Da gaudiorum praemia*, were sung at the coronation, by Cardinal Beaufort, of Henry VI as King of France in Notre-Dame, Paris, December 16th, 1431. (It will be recalled that words of the hymn *Veni Creator*, then as today an essential part of the coronation ritual, are sung complete in the contra-tenor part of Dunstable's motet with that title.)

This hypothesis is rendered more probable because it is known that the king's chapel went to France between April 1430 and the day of the coronation. Henry V's chapel went with him to France from 1417–21, during which time Dunstable was in the service of his brother the Duke of Bedford and Regent of France. The music of many other composers in the Old Hall manuscript was known abroad and they also may have travelled there.

Tinctoris, quoted above as giving high praise to Dunstable, had little regard for his younger contemporaries whom he compares unfavourably with Dufay and Binchois and "the moderns" Okeghem, Busnois, Regis and Caron, "who are the most excellent of all the composers I have ever heard . . . the French contrive music in the newest manner for the new times, while the English continue to use one and the same style of composition, which shows a wretched poverty of invention".

The English composers were certainly conservative in structure but imaginative in detail; but the loss of manuscripts of Masses in the last quarter of the century precludes knowledge of any developments other than the kind of writing found in the Eton Choirbook of large-scale antiphons intended for use in the College chapel. Those that are written for five or more parts show an extension of range of pitch in the highest and lowest parts over the corresponding range of the Old Hall manuscript.

One of the most remarkable pieces in the book, found on its last page, is a setting of the Apostle's Creed for thirteen voices by Robert Wylkynson. The plainsong *cantus firmus,* placed in the top part, consists of the first phrase of the antiphon to the *Magnificat* in the first week in Lent, *Jesus autem transiens.* Below this constantly repeated "refrain" the remaining twelve parts sing the clauses of the Creed in succession in the manner of a *rota,* "each entry being marked in the manuscript with the name of the apostle who was traditionally said to have supplied it. The effect when sung is that the phrase *Jesus autem transiens* has truly passed 'through the midst' and remains at the end". It would be very interesting to hear this novel piece sung.[2]

Another and musically greater work is Richard Davy's setting of the words of the crowd (*turba*) in the St Matthew Passion. The manuscript is unfortunately incomplete, but contains a section worthy to be compared with Bach's treatment of the same words, the awestruck utterance of the centurions *Vere filius Dei erat* ("Truly was this the Son of God"). According to custom the Evangelist's words were sung in plainsong by a tenor, Christ's by a bass, and those of other single persons by an alto. The Evangelist therefore leads into the centurions' words with the sentence "They feared greatly saying", and then follows the four-part setting of their words. It is very simple—but so is Bach's—and the ending, a high and widespread chord, is astonishing as showing a real use of vocal effect. Davy's Passion is the third oldest polyphonic

[2] *Op. cit.,* pp. 413–5.

setting known—all we know of him is that he was organist
of Magdalen College from 1490–2 (the approximate date of
the Eton College manuscript)—the other two, one of a complete Luke Passion for three voices and a part of a Matthew
Passion, being both anonymous and both English.

Two other outstanding composers in this manuscript must
be mentioned, John Browne, whose first setting of *Salve
Regina* in six parts with its sonorous sound and new feeling
for harmonic progression has been likened to "the unfolding
of a flower responding to the sun", and Walter Lambe, a less
dramatic and imaginative composer, whose "wise and experienced mastery is capable of reaching heights both of emotion
and technique". He also composed a fine setting of *Salve
Regina* and followed Dunstable's *Veni sancte Spiritus* in com-
bining two plainsong melodies as a double *cantus firmus*, in
his six-part setting of *O regina caelestis gloriae,* of which
unfortunately only one page has survived.

It is infinitely regrettable that these and other lovely works,
among the greatest glories of our music, should be virtually
unknown to music lovers today. Catholics, especially, should
respond—if they get a chance—to the many settings of votive
antiphons to our Lady and remember that England, Mary's
Dowry, contains more Lady Chapels than any other country
in the world. As Dr Harrison says:

> The votive antiphon . . . was an extra-liturgical form, de-
> tached from the Office though still contained within the frame-
> work of a liturgical *memoria*. It was said by individuals and
> sung in every kind of institution, from the parish guild to the
> college community. Even more than the strictly liturgical forms
> of popular devotion, the Lady Mass and Jesus Mass, the Mary
> antiphon was the universal and characteristic expression of
> the devotional fervour of the later Middle Ages.[3]

This is something that the Coultons and Kensits of this
world will never understand. They regard it from without and

[3] *Op. cit.,* p. 219.

have never, and can never, experience it in its proper perspective.

CAROLS

England, in the fifteenth century, made a distinctive contribution in the shape of the carol: and Volume 4 of *Musica Britannica*, edited by John Stevens, contains over 150 examples, the majority of which are drawn from four different manuscripts. The fact that so many of the carols are found with processional music and marked with liturgical rubrics, led the editor to the conclusion that "in church and out of it the carol was associated with physical movement: when it was not danced to, it was processed to". Another scholar, Dr Harrison, considers the theory that carols were sung in ritual processions is untenable, since the ordinals laid down the chants to be sung for processions throughout the year. Whether or not they were "optional additions to the liturgy" the nature of these carols show them not to be popular by destination, though the carol itself is popular by origin. When the Franciscans arrived in England in the thirteenth century they used songs popular by origin for popular instruction, and the early carols of the century have the characteristic feature of burden and verse which is that of the sophisticated carols in the collection mentioned above. The words of the latter are in English, the mixture of English and Latin called macaronic, or wholly in Latin. The verses are in two, the burdens in three parts throughout or, when there are two burdens, the first is in two and the second in three parts. Burden and verse always alternated.

We associate carols primarily with "the twelve days of Christmas" and so did ecclesiastical authority in the fifteenth century, while the people were inclined to sing them all the year round. There is, however, said to be no trace of the popular monophonic carol—or folk-song—in the collection edited by Dr Stevens. The most familiar carol is the *Agin-*

court Song, composed at the time of the victory of England over France in 1415. Carols for Holy Week, though abundant abroad, are strangely absent from the English repertoire until the late fifteenth and early sixteenth centuries when the passion of our Lord becomes a dominant feature of the texts. Dr Harrison considers these "passion" carols found their place with the household music of the court, and were a part of the late medieval devotion to Jesus which had its liturgical expression in the Jesus Mass and antiphon.

The Wars of the Roses lasted from 1455 to 1485, a strange parallel to the later Thirty Years War in Germany, but infinitely more disastrous to artistic activity in England. Dissatisfaction with the Church, which was becoming increasingly unpopular—as Chaucer and Langland had made apparent—the failure of far-sighted prelates to reform obstinate monastic communities, and of reactionary prelates to control their greed and abjure their worldliness, were all working toward the climax of the anti-papal and anti-clerical revolution in the reign of Henry VIII. The last great pre-Reformation English composer, Robert Fayrfax, born some twenty years before Dunstable's death, lived on to hear "the crash of monastic masonry" resounding throughout the land at a king's command, a king who considered himself orthodox and left large sums of money for Requiem Masses to be said for the repose of his soul—money since diverted to a very different purpose. Wolsey, the typical worldly prelate, took time, in the intervals of destroying monasteries good as well as bad, to admonish the Augustinian Friars to sing devout music "not intended to gratify the ears by the levity of its rhythm, nor to court the approval of worldlings by the multiplicity of its notes, but that in which plainchant raises the minds and the hearts of its hearers to heavenly things", a sentiment expressed before him by St Bernard and many others. Fayrfax, who attended Henry VIII at the Field of the Cloth of Gold and was named at the head of the singers of the Chapel Royal—the one stable musical institution in these troubled years—had been organist of St Albans Priory and composed there his *Missa Regalis* and *Missa Albanus*. The only one of the five extant Masses by Fayrfax not based on a plainsong *cantus firmus* is *O bone Jesu*. In this Mass he drew on his own Jesus-antiphon with the same words and so provides what may be the earliest English example of a Mass connected musically with a polyphonic antiphon.

The most attractive example of Fayrfax's art is the five-part motet *Aeternae laudis lilium,* composed in 1502 at St Albans for the visit of Lady Elizabeth of York. The opening of the motet celebrates "Mary, the lily of eternal praise", and later on mentions her lineage ending with Zacharias and Elizabeth, the parents of John the Baptist. The name of Elizabeth is then taken up by voice after voice with obvious and flattering significance.

It is a pity we do not know more about the way in which the liturgy was carried out in England immediately before the Reformation. In the "Seventy-eight Faults and Abuses of Religion" presented to Henry VIII in 1536 there is talk of "the singing and saying of Mass, Matins or Evensong, as but a roarying, howling, whistleying, mummying, conjuring and jozelying and the playing of the organys a foolish vanitie", but intolerance is obvious in this criticism. Nevertheless the proceedings at the Council of Trent confirm that liturgical observance had become very slack. But if there is abundant evidence of carelessness and irreverence in both sanctuary and nave, we hear all too little of the reverse. The devout and scrupulous made no noise and secured no "headlines". Composers amongst them must have seen with dismay the triumph of Protestantism on the accession of Edward VI (1547) and the replacement of the time-honoured liturgy with a vernacular substitution requiring, at least in some respects, a different kind of music. We shall have occasion to refer to this matter later on.

CHAPTER V

BURGUNDY AND THE

NETHERLANDS

After the Battle of Agincourt and the settling of the English nobility in France, bringing their singers and instrumentalists with them, Paris yielded its supremacy as the chief centre of European music to Cambrai in the province of Hainault, Burgundy, and it was here that Guillaume Dufay (born *c.* 1400) founded the Burgundian school of composers. He sang as a boy in the choir of Cambrai Cathedral, famous for its singing ceremonial and its bells, and he was in the papal choir at Rome in his late twenties and again in 1435. We hear of him in Savoy and Flanders, Florence and Ferrara. The Italian choirs at this time and for some time after were recruited from France and Flanders, and singer-composers of eminence were as eagerly competed for by the courts and churches of Europe as players of football are by various countries today.

Dufay, who became a priest, was made a doctor of canon law in Paris, and when at length he returned to Cambrai he took over the choir. His beautiful music has been described as melancholy and autumnal: but if that description applies to some of his secular polyphonic songs—such as the lovely rondeau *Adieu m'amour*—it cannot be said of his Masses, motets and other church music. "He follows Dunstable aright" as Le Franc's poem put it, and extended that composer's use of the common chord and his expressiveness. One can see the added expressiveness, which some call humanism, in his two lovely settings of the Marian antiphons *Alma Redemptoris Mater* and *Ave Regina Coelorum*, both based on their plainsongs. In the first of these, in three parts (all but the final chords) the embellished plainsong is on the top line and burgeons exquisitely—unaccompanied—in the opening phrase to *Alma*. The other two parts may well have been played on instruments up to (and perhaps including) the held chords at *sumens illud Ave, peccatorum miserere,* each word being separated from the next by a bar's rest. The text of *Ave Regina Coelorum*, in four parts, with the plainsong in the tenor, has tropes inserted for a special purpose. Dufay wrote in his will that he wished the piece to be sung over his death-bed by the members of the Cambrai choir, after he had received the last sacraments, if the hour permitted. The interpolated texts are "Have pity on thy dying Dufay and let him not be cast into the burning fire" and "Have pity, Mother of God, that Heaven's gate may open to the weak one". Dufay's touching request could not be carried out and the piece was sung at his burial. His four-part *L'homme armé* Mass is one of the earliest known examples of the use of this famous fifteenth-century folk-song, a use which continued up to the seventeenth century.

A great deal of unnecessary fuss has been made about the use of secular themes as the *cantus prius factus* in a Mass setting. Only a very sharp and trained ear would have been able to recognize the tune, in the tenor part, with its changed rhythm, added notes and covering polyphony: but in any case no irreverence was intended. On the contrary, it would have been held that the secular melody had been sanctified by its use in church music. Composers, therefore, felt free to use their own secular songs (as Dufay did in his Mass *Si j'ai la face pale*) or other melodic material, indifferent in itself and therefore able to be directed to liturgical ends. Dufay develops further the cyclic Mass—the unifying of the movements by a common theme—and the use of imitation between the parts. There is sometimes more science than appeal in his Masses but the one just mentioned, and the *Caput* Mass based on a melisma at the end of a plainsong antiphon *Venit ad Petrum* sung during the Mandatum (the Washing of the Feet) in Holy Week, are both learned and beautiful. Peter, it will be remembered, asks that Jesus should wash not only his feet but his hands and head (*Non tantum pedes meos, sed et manus et caput*). Dufay's successors Okeghem and Obrecht both composed Masses on this same plainsong melisma. Manfred Bukfozer, in a brilliant chapter of his *Studies in Medieval and Renaissance*, describes how he solved the riddle posed by the single word *Caput*. He found it at last in the antiphon named above in a Sarum Gradual and Processional where it had its origin. It is not found in Roman service books but does occur in several French sources.

In Dufay's later church works the older techniques are fused into a new integrated style; melody is often in the top voice rather than the tenor, four-part varies the three-part writing that had prevailed for so long, modal influence tends to yield to the "atmosphere" of the major and minor scales, though the cadences still avoid the defining leading note, and there is a certain lack of rhythmic vitality.

It is possible that Johannes Okeghem (1430–95) studied with Dufay at Cambrai, certain that he was the outstanding composer of the second half of the fifteenth century until his great pupil, if indeed he was such, Josquin des Prés, born about twenty years later, dominated the entire European musical scene. Okeghem was probably born in Termonde, a district of East Flanders, but spent most of his life in French territory. The diocese of Cambrai extended to Antwerp, and he was a choirboy at the cathedral there for two years. From

1453 onwards he was in charge of the chapel in Paris of Charles VII, king of France, and was appointed also to be treasurer of the Abbey of St Martin in Tours, a post that was much sought after because of its financial rewards. He was, therefore, a wealthy and also a much respected man. His death called forth a rhymed lament, 400 verses long, from the poet Guillaume Cretin, a piece in Latin in his praise from Erasmus, and a beautiful motet of mourning from Josquin des Prés. Okeghem, like one of his most eminent pupils Jacob Obrecht (c. 1430–1505), excelled in his Masses, while Josquin, as we shall see, excelled in his motets.

Okeghem brought a harmonic strength and virility into his church music that was lacking in Dufay. Gothic complexities certainly find a place in his work though his famous motet for thirty-six voices has only eighteen real parts. Like Dufay he based some of his Masses on secular polyphonic songs including a number by himself. Thus one of his finest Masses is based on his ballade *Fors seulement,* another on a lovely polyphonic song by Gilles Binchois (c. 1400–60) *De plus en plus*: but his masterpiece is the *Caput* Mass, on the plainsong melisma used by Dufay. He uses imitation more subtly than his predecessors and one of the features of his musical diction is, as Ernst Krenek describes it in his monograph on the composer,[1]

an unusual and at times bewildering continuity. . . . Just as his melodic phrases seem to be suspended in mid-air because of the indefinite, ever shifting, and unpredictable location of their points of emphasis, so his music rolls on for long stretches without clearly discernible stopping points . . . it is as if a very long bridge were to be built without pillars: each time a span was completed, at the point where a supporting pillar would normally be required, some miraculous engineering device would cause another span to issue from it, and thus the process would continue until the opposite shore was reached.

[1] Ernest Krenek, *Johannes Ockeghem,* Sheed and Ward, London, 1953.

This continuous melodic writing, needless to say, makes great demands on the singers. Okeghem's Requiem Mass is the oldest polyphonic setting extant, Dufay's having apparently been lost. He uses throughout the paraphrase technique on the plainsong themes and ends at the Offertory, the rest being sung in plainsong. At this period the text of the Proper of the Mass for the Dead varied from one locality to another, and in France the Tract, *Absolve Domine* in the present liturgy, was replaced by *Sicut cervus* (a conflation of two psalm texts). Pierre de la Rue († 1518), born in Picardy or Tournai, in his Requiem, which includes also polyphony for *Sanctus, Agnus Dei* and Communion, has made a particularly beautiful setting of *Sicut cervus*. Okeghem's Marian motets, including *Alma Redemptoris Mater* and two settings of *Salve Regina,* are among the most accessible of his works for modern ears. These Flemish composers treat the Mass and motet in many and various ways and, of course, have recourse to many of the same borrowed themes. Thus Obrecht uses *L'homme armé* or *Caput,* as Dufay and Okeghem had done, and draws on his own motets, and also on chansons of and before his time. In his later work the features of the so-called "parody Mass" appear. This is a Mass which does not merely use a single borrowed melody, or a paraphrase of it, but draws on all the polyphonic parts of its model. It is a type of Mass very prominent in the sixteenth century. Obrecht's harmony looks to the future in such works as his beautiful setting of the *Pater Noster,* predominantly chordal and with well defined and non-modal cadences. In his *Missa sine nomine* (that is a freely composed work without any borrowed material) he shows a considerable feeling for vocal effect.

Composers, up to the end of the sixteenth century, but less often afterwards, poured into the chief art form of their time, the five-movement Mass[2] (the equivalent of the symphony)

---

[2] Taking *Sanctus-Benedictus* as one movement.

and the motet (the equivalent of the tone-poem) their highest skill, *ad majorem Dei gloriam,* for the glory also of music and natural joy in the exercise of their talent: but one must not lose sight of the simplicity of some of their smaller pieces or even some simple sections in complicated works. There is, for example, an exquisitely simple setting of the poignant words *O vos omnes* (so familiar in Victoria's superb setting) by Loyset Compère († 1518), singer-in-ordinary to Charles VIII, and later canon and chancellor at St Quentin.

We come now to the great Josquin des Prés of whom Luther, no mean judge, said that "other composers do what they can with the notes, Josquin alone does what he wishes". If this is, to some extent, a prejudiced comment it is true that Josquin's mastery over his material is supreme. He can and did indulge in highly complicated structures, especially in the earlier part of his career, but Italy, yet again, worked a spell on him and the music he wrote under that spell speaks to us as if it had just come fresh from his pen. Donald Tovey said, in a lecture on music to members of the British Academy in 1938: "For me the main stream of music becomes navigable at the end of the fifteenth century with such composers as Josquin des Prés, and remains smoothly navigable throughout the sixteenth century. At the beginning of the seventeenth century it enters regions partly mountainous and partly desert, and becomes choked with weeds."

This is not a view any musical historian could possibly take, nor one that most musicians would take without many reservations today, but it is one that for sheer lack of experience or lack of the "historical" ear and imagination, many music lovers do take. To them plainsong is monotonous and polyphony a difficult web of colourless sound. This attitude can easily be combated, but one must allow that all true church music serving liturgical ideals is functional and, as has been said before, out of place in the concert hall or anywhere but in church where it is placed in the proper tempo of Mass or Office. That is not to say it cannot be enjoyed outside these conditions, but not in the highest degree due to it. It is depressing to contemplate the huge bulk of church music that had been written up to the point this book has now reached and to realize how much of it one will never hear. It is indeed not dead—but it sleeps all too soundly.

Before speaking of Josquin's church music a word must be said about the impact, or otherwise, of the Renaissance. It is hard to find any trace of what the Renaissance means in terms of the visual arts or literature in the church music of the period it is supposed to cover—let us say from about 1400 to 1600.

Parallels are often drawn between architecture and church music and can be illuminating up to a point. One can find in the lines of Romanesque architecture a certain parallel with plainsong but it can be found equally well in a Norman arch, or a Gothic vault as simple as that of Salisbury Cathedral, while the complexities of "Gothic music" that we have encountered can be paralleled by the intricate interiors of, let us say, Amiens Cathedral or King's College Chapel—but also in the elaborate decorations in the Lindisfarne Gospel painted c. 700, or for that matter in a Persian carpet.

Nothing in plainsong can be equated with such medieval illuminations, and nothing in Renaissance art, it seems to the author, can be equated with church music during the conventional period stated above. Those gorgeous ceilings and decorations in the Roman basilicas, the writhing columns of Bernini's baldachino in St Peter's, the all too human ecstasy of his St Teresa, what equivalents do such things have in the liturgy or the music written for it by any of the composers we have dealt with, or in the music of Palestrina, Victoria, Lassus or Byrd, the last great composers of Catholic church music?

If this verdict is in any way true, where then did sacred music go to in emerging from the Middle Ages? The answer to that might be that it passed into the great classical age of such music, a fusion of the medieval and the modern. One can, of course, put painters and musicians side by side, as for example Josquin and Raphael, Palestrina and Fra Angelico, Victoria and El Greco—but we shall not get much beyond imperfect analogies between painters' and musicians' lines, rhythms and colours.

Before returning to Josquin and his later contemporaries mention must be made of the very important invention of the printing of music which took place in *c.* 1470; the earliest known example of printing from movable type being a Roman Missal with the lozenge-shaped notes of the plainsong in black, the staves in red. The most outstanding name here is that of Ottaviano dei' Petrucci whose position as a printer of music, Reese says, is analogous to that of Gutenberg as a printer of books. It was possible to circulate music now, whether plainsong, polyphony or musical illustrations in theoretical books, over a much wider area than could be covered by the manuscripts of the past, such as the exquisite Squarcialupi Codex, which can be seen in the Medicean Library at Florence. Squarcialupi was succeeded in his post as organist at the cathedral by Heinrich Isaac, who numbered among his pupils the three talented sons of Lorenzo de' Medici. Isaac, born at Brabant (East Flanders) *c.* 1450, became, in 1479, court composer to Emperor Maximilian, another great patron of art, at Vienna and remained in his service until his death in Florence in 1517. He was allowed to go there because the emperor said "he will be more useful to us at Florence than at our own court", by which he meant politically useful. It is sad that Isaac is known today chiefly by a keyboard arrangement of a song with words said to have been written by the emperor, *Innsbruck, ich muss dich lassen,* the melody of which was freely adapted as a Lutheran chorale and introduced by Bach into the St Matthew Passion (*Ich bin's, ich sollte bussen*). Isaac's greatest work is the monumental *Choralis Constantinus* (so-called because commissioned, in 1508, by the cathedral chapter at Constance). It is the first polyphonic setting of the whole of the Proper texts of the Mass for all Sundays of the Church's year and some saints' days. The settings are mainly in four parts with the plainsong melody usually in the treble in Books I–II, but in the bass in Book III. Reese calls the work a *tour de force* of Netherlandish technique. Present-day liturgical observance, which demands that the Proper be sung in plainsong, prevents this work being heard in church. Isaac is the first international composer in the sense that, like Lassus in later years, he set Italian, German and French words.

We are also unlikely to hear the *Missa Cucu* by Johannes Martini, a Flemish composer from Armentières who taught Isabella d'Este singing. In the final clause of the *Gloria* (*Patris, Amen*) in his *Cucu* Mass the bird's minor third call is heard in the alto part at three different pitch levels.

Josquin, as we have seen, was born *c*. 1450 at Condé-sur-l'Escaut, a Fleming by birth, but in every other way a Frenchman. In 1491 he was in the service of Cardinal Ascanio Sforza at Milan and in consequence became nicknamed Josquin d'Ascanio. From 1486–94 Josquin sang, with some interruptions, in the papal choir at Rome and five years later the archives showed him to be in the employ—as Martini had been—of Duke Ercole of Ferrara. We next find him as master of the chapel of Louis XII until the king's death in 1515, and at length back in his birthplace where he remained until his death in 1521. There is evidence to show that he was a man of independent character. Duke Ercole's secretary, recommending the engagement of Isaac instead of Josquin, complains that though the latter was the best composer "he does it when it suits him and not when one wishes him to". His fame spread far and wide and Gaspar Siciliano, a noted singer of the day, then at the court of Urbino, reports "when a motet was sung recently in the presence of the duchess no one seemed to like it, no one had anything to say in praise of it, until it became known it was by Josquin des Prés". A familiar example of artistic snobbery!

Josquin dominates and sums up the whole of an era—both of secular as well as of sacred music. He had every scientific process at his finger-tips and could also write with extra-ordinary simplicity. His was the art that conceals art. It has been said that he was at his greatest in his motets. In *Vultum tuum deprecabuntur*, for example, a motet in seven parts, he perfectly unites science and expression, but the length of the piece is against its performance today. Much more viable are two wonderful motets devoted to our Lady, *Salve Regina* and *Ave Maria, virgo serena*. The first of these, for five voices, begins with the first four notes of the Marian antiphon given out by treble, tenor and alto successively, and thereafter heard only in the alto part on two pitches, while the complete plain-song melody appears, in decorated form, in the top voice. This motet was published by Andreas Antiquus, a contempor-ary of Petrucci, in 1521 with the "motto" theme marked "who persists shall be saved".

The *Ave Maria*, for four voices, has a paraphrase of the text of one of the many Sequences regrettably jettisoned by the Council of Trent. Josquin uses canon in it with great art and indeed in one of the "panels" of this lovely picture *Ave vera virginitas*—which is often sung by itself—the ordinary listener would not notice that soprano and tenor sing the exquisite folk-songlike melody in canon. Another canon, this time between treble and bass, with a sequence of three phrases of rising thirds, makes a beautiful effect. The whole piece is one of the glories of polyphony. Another very simple and much shorter motet for voices, *Tu solus, qui facis mirabilia* (a text from an old French Breviary not in use in the liturgy today) shows Josquin's use of sustained chordal writing. The second part contains a brief quotation from a French song by Okeghem: this brings to mind Josquin's fine *Déploration*

(Lament) on the death of his teacher. An intensity of pathos hitherto unknown to music comes into his setting of David's lament for Saul and Jonathan, *Planxit autem David,* in which the composer paraphrases the well-known plainsong tone, in all four parts, for the Lamentations of Jeremiah in Holy Week with most moving effect, and into David's lament for his son Absalom, *Absalom fili mi,* a remarkably dramatic piece. And so one could continue ranging through this wonderful series of motets. One must mention two larger scale works, *Stabat Mater* which, like Palestrina's setting, is predominantly chordal, and *Miserere Mei Deus* (Psalm 50) composed for the duke of Ferrara. This motet is based on the recitation formula of the first half of a psalm tone and is remarkable for the descent in Part 1 and ascent in Part 2 of this motive over an octave.

In his *Missa Hercules Dux Ferrarie* Josquin paid homage to an earthly as well as heavenly ruler for the *cantus firmus* is formed out of the vowels of Duke Ercole's title in Latin which, with some manipulation, gives in sol-fa syllables *re, ut, re, ut, re, re, fa, mi, re,* not a very inspiring theme but used with considerable ingenuity: and if, as may have been the case, it was played on a brass instrument, one that could blaze out with gratifying power at the appropriate points in the *Gloria* (e.g. *cujus regni non erit finis*) and the final clause of the *Credo,* where it is twice repeated in short order rising successively a fifth and a fourth. The *Benedictus* of *Sanctus* is divided into three variously scored duets with the theme always in the tenor—which, in the second duet, is the top part.

The fine flower of Josquin's Masses—for the *Hercules* is an early work—can be found in such lovely works as the *Missa da pacem,* with a plainsong *cantus firmus, Da pacem in diebus nostris,* in the tenor, but permeating the other voices. The first three movements and the first *Agnus* all begin with the same three-part polyphony, soprano and bass repeating the first three notes of the *cantus firmus* given out by the alto.

The second *Agnus* and the third (scored for six voices) contain fine canonic writing.

How expressive Josquin can be is shown in the moving *Et incarnatus est* section of the *Credo*, scored mainly in the black chords which he so much favoured. The Mass *Pange lingua* is a masterly paraphrase of the glorious plainsong hymn in which, as in the previous Mass, every movement begins with a reference to the plainsong and then weaves it into all the parts with exquisite art, and in which the *Et incarnatus est* is this time wholly chordal. The *Hosanna in excelsis* of the *Sanctus* dances along in triple measure.

Perhaps one day the superb music of this very great master, sacred and secular, will become better known. He sums up the whole art of the Netherland school; and while his technical skill amazes, it is the tonal beauty and expressive richness of his music and his close attention to his texts that are the truly appealing features of his works.

Among his pupils Gombert must have brief mention. More than a quarter of his motets are devoted to our Lady and these include one that quotes seven different Marian plainsong melodies, six of which can be found in the *Liber Usualis*. These are *Alma Redemptoris Mater, Salve Regina, Ave Regina, Ave Maria, Beata Mater* and *Inviolata*; the seventh has a text from the Song of Songs, *Hortus conclusus*. These melodies are reshaped in various ways so as to fit together, four being usually sung at the same time.

CHAPTER VI

THE COUNCIL OF TRENT[1]

Calls for the reform of church music had been voiced by popes, Councils and individuals for at least a century before the Council of Trent met. We shall learn on p. 104 what Pope Marcellus said to the Sistine Chapel Choir when he rebuked their behaviour and the kind of music they sang and one of his charges, that the words of the liturgy must be intelligible, was also one of the chief recommendations, together with the elimination of secular melodies, in the decrees of the 22nd Session, September 17th, 1562. The Council was concerned with fundamental attitudes, not specifically musical problems, but even so its influence was far-reaching. The words that anything "lascivious or impure" whether by instrument or voice could not be tolerated referred mainly to the associations of the melodies used, that is, to the words to which they were sung: a situation paralleled by the attitude of the Fathers of the Church towards profane music. The congregation, if they recognized the secular melody, might well also remember the words. The organ came under strong criticism also and (evidently the habit still lingers on) organists were prone to play for far too long a time and too noisily, even introducing dance tunes and so "assuring more titillation than devotion". The

[1] For the facts and extracts from documents translated into English in this section I am deeply indebted to two articles in *The Musical Quarterly*: "Church Music and the Council of Trent", by K. G. Fellerer (October, 1953) and "Vincenzo Ruffo and Musical Reform after the Council of Trent", by Lewis H. Lockwood (July, 1957).

organ should be silent "from the elevation of the Host to the *Agnus Dei,* during which interval the thoughts of all should contemplate in deep silence the passion of our Lord and our redemption". These criticisms were constantly repeated by the Council of Trent, and by other Councils and Synods.

It becomes clear also that the *Gloria* and *Credo* in the Mass were sometimes not sung, a display on the organ of "frivolous or sometimes wicked melodies" being provided instead while the celebrant, presumably, read the words *sotto voce.* "Fancy music", vocal and instrumental, was heard even during Holy Week, to which "all the young people of either sex eagerly flock together, and experience has shown that sins and scandals no less heinous have been committed". The Feast of Fools, and other such "buffooneries" that aroused "giggling and immoderate laughter" were forbidden by the Concilium Senonesse, 1528; but the most vivid description, possibly exaggerated, of the licence of music comes in a tract *De incertitudine et vanitate scientiarum et artium,* Cologne, 1532.

> Today music has such great licence in churches that even along with the canon of the Mass certain obscene little ditties sometimes have equal share; and even the divine offices themselves and the sacred prayers and petitions are performed by lascivious musicians hired at great price, not to make the hearers understand or for the elevation of the spirit, but to incite wanton prurience, not with human voices but with the cries of beasts: boys whining the descant, some bellow the tenor, others bark the counterpoint, others gnash the alto, others moo the bass: the result is that a multitude of sounds is heard, but of the words and prayers not a syllable is understood; the authority of judgement is withdrawn from ears and mind alike.

Bishop Cirillo Franco was one of the most outspoken of the reactionary critics of the current techniques of Mass and motet composition and voices his views forcibly in a letter of 1549. Though not professing to be a musician it seems to him that composers have sacrificed spiritual significance to technical skill, that they have turned their back on the appeal of the ancient modes and the diversity of the earlier age of polyphony.

Today all these things (individual sections of Masses and motets) which are so different from one another are sung in the same tone and the same mode. [Turning to the use of secular themes he asks] what the devil has music to do with the armed man or with the nightingale or with the Duke of Ferrara? [Entering the field of secular modern music he finds nothing good, compared with the past] except the pavanne and the galliard. [He comes out strongly against fugues:] Today all musicians place their beatitude in forcing the singing into the fugal form, so that one singer says *Sanctus* another says *Sabaoth,* and the third *Gloria tua* with shouts and garglings, so that they seem more like cats in January than flowers in May.

It would have greatly distressed the good bishop had he been able to foresee that "fugal form" was to get such a grip on certain sections of the *Gloria, Credo* and *Sanctus* in the eighteenth century and onwards, a practice that led, even with some great composers, to stiff and dull music: but perhaps he would have deplored the convention of showing particular contrapuntal skill in *Agnus Dei,* which became one of the glories of Palestrina's music. Franco, in his insistence that the marking of the meaning of the words is the only justification for church music—in which he is quite right—may often be unfair to contemporary composers but he did not deny them "some good invention and discernment".

Franco found an opponent, a hundred years later, in King John IV of Portugal (1604–56), who pointed out that music could not live on the past. The composer of church music must be accorded freedom to write in the idiom of his time, as he does in secular music and, it amounts to this, the art of the composer was to enrich the liturgy as well as to make as intelligible as possible what was sung. The ideal of the Council was, of course, intelligibility first and foremost, but apparently this could not be unless counterpoint was entirely abjured, and unless church music followed the harmonic revolution of the seventeenth century—with which we shall be dealing in a later section of this book. We see therefore polyphony in combat with homophony, counterpoint with chords.

The "modernists" of the new generation, summing up the Masses that pleased the Council and the ideals they represented, spoke of Palestrina's "barbaric productions" and as unfavourably of Josquin, etc. The new church art, they considered, was to be monodic, the *stile moderno*, not the *stile antico*.

Giovanni Baptista Doni (1594–1647) wrote: "I am still surprised at the famous music of Palestrina which so pleased the reverend gentlemen and which brought it about that the Council of Trent did not banish music from the Church: for if this music is still valued, it is not for use but to be preserved and cared for in some museum, like a fine antique." It is amusing to recall that Joannes Tinctoris (*c*. 1435–1511), a chaplain to Ferdinand I, at Naples, celebrated theorist and compiler of our earliest dictionary of musical terms, had the same contemptuous attitude towards the Flemish music of the past. "It is only during the last forty years", he writes in 1477, "that there have been compositions which, according to the judgement of the experts, are worth hearing." It is an odd and often repeated story of ignorance of the past.

By the *Motu proprio Alias nonnullas constitutiones* of Pius IV, August 2nd, 1564, eight cardinals were charged with carrying out the resolutions of the Council of Trent, which had closed eight months before. Two of these cardinals were Vitellozzo Vitellozzi and St Charles Borromeo. Disciplinary reform was their immediate task, one of its results being the dismissal of fourteen members of the papal chapel; but the establishment of a style of sacred music conformable to the general findings of the Council was the next step, as difficult as it was important. We are, fortunately, well informed about the action the highly cultured Cardinal Borromeo took in the matter as, owing to his having to be in Rome instead of in his own diocese of Milan, he corresponded frequently with Nicolo Ormaneto of Verona who acted as his vicar general in the Milan diocese. He writes, on January 6th, 1565, that "he is glad to hear some qualified person has been found to teach the students of the seminary the Ambrosian chant and rite" and similarly the other master for figured music. The latter was most probably Vincenzo Ruffo who was to play a prominent part in realizing the ideals of church music the Council had in mind and which was still being debated. Ruffo, according to the researches of Lewis H. Lockwood, was born earlier than had previously been assumed, c. 1520, "with a likely date centring around 1505", and so on his second removal from Verona to Milan in 1563, he would have been nearly sixty years old. He was now to change the hitherto conservative style of his sacred music, which is sharply defined from the progressive tendencies of his madrigals. As Mr Lockwood says: "In this new and prominent position (as master of the chapel of Milan Cathedral) the approximately sixty-year-old composer now found himself director of music at the largest cathedral of northern Italy, the central basilica of the Ambrosian rite, and a seat of religious activity whose leaders could clearly sense impending reform."

Borromeo wrote to his vicar from Rome on March 10th, 1565: "I desire above all that the matter of the intelligible music succeeds according to the hope you have given me. Therefore I would like you to order Ruffo, in my name, to compose a Mass which should be as clear as possible and send it to me here." This request indicates that Ormaneto had suggested Ruffo for the purpose. At the end of the month Cardinal Borromeo inquires if Don Nicola (Vincentino) "who favours chromatic music" would also compose a Mass, "thus by the comparison of the work of many excellent musicians we will better be able to judge this intelligible music". This request is a tribute to the great cardinal's liberality of mind for Vincentino was a "modernist", as the allusion to chromatic music implies, but in a treatise "The old music accommodated to modern practice" he had urged that the treatment of the Mass and motet should be different from that of *canzoni francese* or madrigals; it must be "serious and not greatly agitated, not based on secular themes which turn the temple of God into a stage where it is permissible to perform every kind of music of a ridiculous and ludicrous buffoonery". Unfortunately there is no Mass extant by Vincentino, nor do we know what Masses were performed, in April, 1565, when the papal singers assembled at the house of Cardinal Vitellozzi, at his request, "to demonstrate whether the words could be understood".

The account of Baini, published in 1828, has long since been discredited, though it is given further currency in Pfitzner's noble opera *Palestrina*; in that work Borromeo orders Palestrina to produce the required Mass and when he refuses has him put into prison. There he is visited by angels who obligingly dictate the music of the Pope Marcellus Mass (composed, in fact, before the Council of Trent convened) to him: Baini does not mention the other Masses sung on this historic occasion. Palestrina's work might well have been performed, as also Masses by such eminent men as Lassus and Animuccia—perhaps also the putative Mass by Vincentino—and surely the Mass Borromeo commissioned from Ruffo, which may well be one of the four in the first collection published in 1570, after his appointment at Milan Cathedral. The dedication to the Milanese Senator Antonello Arcimboldo "a literary man of a strong religio-humanistic turn, and apparently at least an amateur of music", bears out this assumption. After alluding to Borromeo's commission

and its reason—to obey the decree of the Council of Trent—
he continues:

> You . . . as it were showed me the prototype of this manner
> of composing music. Accordingly guided by your help, I com-
> posed *one Mass* in this way; so that the number of the syllables
> and the voices and tones together should be clearly and dis-
> tinctly understood and perceived by the pious listeners. Thus
> it was that *later imitating that example* I more readily and
> easily composed other Masses of the same type [italics Mr
> Lockwood's].

The obvious difficulty that Ruffo had to face was how to
replace the well-tried devices of the imitation of one part by
another, the "fugal form" denounced by Bishop Franco, and
the individual rhythms of each part that had lent such vitality
to the Palestrinian style. Composers in that style, and before
it—in the sacred music of Dufay and Josquin for example—
had written purely chordal passages for special moments of
solemnity or jubilation, but now that verbal clarity was to be
the overriding factor such chordal passages had to become
the norm, and that is what we find in the 1570 book of Ruffo's
Masses which—as has been said—probably include one sung
to the cardinals. But inevitably a compromise had to be
reached, and it was reached much in the same manner as in
William Byrd's "short" and "great" services for the Anglican
Church, composed *c.* 1606, when the demand for clarity, and
one note to one syllable, was made by the Reformers. Ruffo
himself introduced greater rhythmic freedom, and small
groups of notes as embellishments of cadence points, and
unifying motives between movements, and so forth. In the
later Masses of 1574 Ruffo considered he had come closest
to achieving the intentions of the holy Fathers "who some
years ago, in the city of Trent, gave the world such Christian
doctrine and such holy laws".

As Mr Lockwood points out "Ruffo's achievement stands
quite outside the Palestrinian orbit: for the latter's renewed

emphasis on contrapuntal procedures, refined in the highest degree, bespeaks a conservatism markedly different from his own": he has nothing in common with the brilliant polychoral style, certainly predominantly homophonic, of the Venetian masters, such as the Gabrielis, but a decided kinship with the northern Italian Mass style found, pre-eminently, in the works of Gian Matteo Asola, of which, as of others of that school, we speak elsewhere. The fact is that music could not be shackled to the degree required by the Council of Trent, but that does not detract from the valiant efforts made to purge sacred music of the bad ways it had adopted.

Mass music was to suffer further indignities in the seventeenth and eighteenth centuries until called to order by the famous *Motu proprio* of Pius X, who built on the findings of the Council. Even the reform of plainsong, so imperfectly carried out in the Medicean edition of 1614, and propagated in the Ratisbon edition of 1871–81, was to lead to the great reform of Solesmes and the Vatican official edition of 1903.

Few composers, probably, worked with such single-minded devotion as Ruffo in trying to realize the style of sacred music desired by the Council of Trent and his master Cardinal Borromeo, and it is touching to read that when the aged composer, then a badly paid choirmaster in a little town in Forli, far removed from the central areas of musical life, came, in the Holy Year of 1575, on a pilgrimage to Rome with his musical company he received special recognition from Gregory XIII which must have immensely consoled him. "As the pilgrims passed two and two to kiss the toe of Gregory, the pope, knowing Ruffo was amongst them, said, 'When he passes, tell me, for I wish to see him', and when he passed the pope embraced and kissed him."

CHAPTER VII

THE SIXTEENTH CENTURY

THE ROMAN SCHOOL

We shall be concerned here with the tremendous upheaval caused by the Reformation—which began *c*. 1520 in Germany and Switzerland and spread through Northern and Western Europe—in two matters only, the challenge presented to the Catholic Church by the emergence of a vernacular liturgy among the Protestants and Luther's potent words, "Let the people sing". No way could be found of meeting this challenge really effectively, for obvious reasons, and the Church has been unable to discover a satisfactory way of doing so without surrendering the Latin liturgy. Luther, with the aid of his disciples, gave his followers melodies to sing taken from folksongs, part-songs, plainsong adaptations of hymns and melodies newly composed; the whole eventually forming a huge treasury of popular song. At the same time he did not abjure polyphony—we have seen how much he admired Josquin—and he made free use of what suited his purpose. A motet was habitually sung in the Lutheran Mass. Plainsong never got into the bloodstream of the people as did the chorale; its use in polyphony made no appeal to them because they did not, in general, notice its presence, whereas the chorale was immediately recognizable. It is true that it could become, as in many of Bach's cantatas and organ works, decorated and thematically developed beyond the ordinary man's recognition, but one has only to hear the entry of the chorale "O

Lamb of God" unembellished, in (to give a very familiar example) the opening chorus of the St Matthew Passion, to realize how profound must have been its appeal and with what emotion the people joined in the harmonized chorales.

The Lutheran movement, the terrible sack of Rome in 1527, when the dreaded German and Swiss mercenaries pillaged the city and attacked Leo X and the French invaded Italy at Genoa and marched to Naples expecting to fight the Germans there, made the times wholly unpropitious for any such thing as the rise of a Roman school of composers. But the arrival of Adrian Willaert in the independent and relatively untroubled Republic of Venice, where he was appointed choirmaster at St Mark's in 1527, signalized the beginning of the transformation of Netherland into Northern Italian church music, based on the former and culminating through a line of great composers in the immense achievement of Monteverdi.

Palestrina

In Rome the Franco-Netherlanders dominated the choirs of the Sistine and the Julian Chapels and it was not until the latter part of the sixteenth century that the decisive change began that made Rome, with Venice as rival, the new centre of the musical world. By this time the Counter-Reformation, in which the Society of Jesus, founded by St Ignatius Loyola, and formally approved by Paul III in 1540, played a prominent part, was on the move and the Council of Trent (1545–63) had begun its long deliberations. In either 1524 or 1525 Giovanni Pierluigi had been born into the small hill town of Palestrina, which he added to his name. He is listed, without a date, among the singing boys of the Liberian chapel in St Mary Major and probably studied under Arcadelt in Rome. In 1544 he became organist and choirmaster at his home cathedral of which, fortunately for him, the future pope, Julius III, was the bishop. This pope appointed the brilliantly gifted young man master of the Julian Chapel over the heads of its other members and in gratitude Palestrina composed and dedicated to him the Mass on the plainsong *cantus firmus Ecce Sacerdos magnus*. The volume of Masses in which it appears, the first he had published, brings us the earliest portrait of the composer who is shown, in a frontispiece, on his knees presenting it to the pope, who is blessing him. A tiny woodcut of the pope's coat-of-arms is placed beside the plainsong theme every time it appears in the Mass. Delighted with this gift Julius made Palestrina, in 1555, a member of the pontifical choir in spite of his having a poor tenor voice, being married—which was forbidden—and there being no vacancy.

Three months later the pope died and was succeeded by Marcellus II, whose reign only lasted three weeks: but in that time an event took place which had a profound effect on Palestrina. After the Good Friday ceremonies in the Sistine Chapel were over the pope summoned the singers to his presence and rebuked them for the casual way they had performed the liturgy. He ended his speech with the pregnant remark that "everything should be both heard and understood properly". It was, doubtless, these words and the early death of the holy old man that made Palestrina resolve to compose the famous Mass that bears the pope's name.

The austere Paul IV, who succeeded Marcellus, included the papal choir in his programme of reforms when, to his dismay, he discovered that several of its members were married men with families, whereas it was the strict rule that they should be single, and where possible in minor orders so as to be able to take part in the reading of certain sections of the liturgy. He further found that some of the singers had been composing secular pieces, such as madrigals, then a novelty. Palestrina, who was married, had a family, and had not only published a book of madrigals but styled himself a member of the papal choir, was naturally among those dismissed. But he soon obtained the post of musical director at

St John Lateran, the cathedral church of Rome, and remained there for five years, perhaps composing the *Missa Papae Marcelli* and *Missa Brevis* during this period and, for certain, one set of the *Lamentations*. The manuscript of part of these in his own hand is one of the great treasures of the Lateran.

Badly paid and not at all happy he seems, judging by an entry in the minute-book of the chapter, to have "gone off at a moment's notice". In March 1561 he returned as master of the choir to St Mary Major, where he had been a chorister, and remained there for about six years during which time he acquired a valuable and wealthy patron in Cardinal Ippolito d'Este at whose lovely villa he spent some part of each year. At length, after flirting with the idea of entering the service of the Emperor Maximilian II as director of music at the Court of Vienna, he was appointed director of the Julian choir at St Peter's, at a salary larger than that of his predecessor Animuccia: and in 1571 he moved to the house near St Peter's where he died, on the feast of the Purification, February 2nd, 1594.

Much has been made of the fact that Palestrina after his wife's death in 1580, having made up his mind to study for the priesthood and receiving the tonsure, changed direction and married a well-to-do widow who had inherited a prosperous skin and furrier business; and not only went into the business himself but did well in it. Posterity should be glad of his decision, even if the immediate motive, security, was not a very worthy one, for the money he now had at his disposal enabled him to publish sixteen collections of various works, many of which might otherwise have been lost to us.

How highly regarded Palestrina was by his contemporaries was shown in a tribute organized by Giovanni Asola of Verona and thirteen other composers in Venetia, Lombardy and Tuscany, in the form of a collection of psalm settings for Vespers composed by them, bearing a laudatory dedication and accompanied by a letter in which Asola compared this prince of music "to an ocean of knowledge" and others to "rivers whose life is bound up with the sea, into which they shed their tribute".

One does not readily associate Palestrina with a sense of humour but he replied to this effusion with a short setting of a Vespers antiphon of which the words were, "Ye are my friends, if ye do what I teach, saith the Lord"!

The singling out of Palestrina as not only the one composer of his time worth consideration or, even more foolishly, as "the first great composer of sacred music" has naturally produced a corresponding reaction. Some musicologists now speak of him as inferior to Josquin, Lassus and Byrd, and even as practising a decadent art. He lived, as his contemporaries did, in the sunset time of sacred polyphony: but decadence is found not in his music but in that of those who, especially in the Cecilian movement of the nineteenth century, tried to copy him with disastrous results. He was not an abler craftsman than his great contemporaries any more than they, or he, were abler than Josquin: but he is, surely indisputably, the greatest exponent in church music of the true liturgical spirit, and this precisely because of the severe limitations he imposed upon himself and his reasons, which he made explicit, for doing so. In his preface to his motets or spiritual madrigals on texts from the Song of Songs he writes that he blushes at and grieves for the love-songs (that is his secular madrigals) that he had written and published. This preface has been dismissed as blatantly hypocritical: but, in his admirable book on the composer,[1] Dr Henry Coates comes near to the truth in suggesting that it was Palestrina's full realization of his mission as a church composer that made him write in this vein. It certainly was that realization that led him to take what one might call musical vows of poverty, obedience and chastity.

[1] Master Musician series.

The serene and supple beauty of Palestrina's melodic lines (called by Debussy "divine arabesques") show their affinity to plainsong and go down, as Dr Coates says, into its subsoil. His melodic "poverty" shows in the restricted range of intervals he used, his harmonic "poverty" in the employment mainly of common chords and their first inversions, his "obedience" in the subjection of not only accented but unaccented notes to strict rules in regard to dissonance and consonance, rules rarely departed from, his "chastity" in an expression which accords with the spirit of the liturgical text. But while proportion, sobriety and serenity, a perfect equilibrium between the two dimensions of the vertical and the horizontal, are among the chief characteristics of Palestrina's art, he must not be thought of as emasculated, devoid of emotion, or over-rarefied. What Edward Fitzgerald said of Mozart could also be said of Palestrina: "People cannot believe Mozart is powerful because he is so beautiful."

In his music there is "purity of style, the coupling of ideal contents with ideal form". Victoria is emotionally more moving, Lassus and Byrd more adventurous and various; but Pius X was absolutely right in singling out Palestrina in his *Motu proprio* of 1909 as having, from the liturgical point of view, reached the greatest perfection in the classic polyphony of the sixteenth century and approaching nearest to Gregorian chant, "the supreme model for sacred music".

Palestrina composed 105 Masses (if there are included the ten, alternating plainsong and polyphony, written for Mantua in accordance with the practice there) and 400 to 500 motets, including under that heading settings of hymns, the Magnificat, Litanies, etc. Lassus composed the staggering figure of 516 motets, including the Penitential Psalms, etc. And when there is added the considerable output of sacred music by the other outstanding sixteenth-century composers, let alone those of lesser rank, the mind of the unfortunate author, trying to give a reasonably clear (but hardly comprehensive!) picture of their achievement, begins to reel.

It is, of course, true that these composers spoke an international musical language, even though one coloured by national traits, and used the same assortment of technical devices, varying these with astonishing skill. To the inexperienced ear their music may all "sound alike", just as would that of the preceding century. But as Obrecht is different from Okeghem, so *mutatis mutandis* is, let us say, Palestrina from Lassus.

Distinctive features of Palestrina's style are the almost mathematical balance of phrases, the scoring of common chords so as to give them maximum sonority, and a love of conjunct motion. How hard he worked to secure intelligibility of the text in his Masses can be shown in comparing the early, deliberately academic Mass *Ad fugam* (composed at a time when he was accused of showing "more fantasy than learning"—that is writing in too chordal a style) and the Mass of Pope Marcellus. Dr Jeppeson in his fine study *Palestrina and the Dissonance* has worked out the number of times that the same syllables coincide in the *Gloria* of the Masses, thus not obscuring the text: and the number of times that they do not. Thus the Marcellus shows 204 cases to only 8 in *Ad fugam* of coinciding syllables, and only 31 to 203 of different syllables entering simultaneously in various voices. The Mass *Assumpta est Maria*, of a later date, is the next in clarity to the *Marcellus*. Forty-four of Palestrina's Masses are of the parody type, that is based on a pre-existing model (motet or other material), 31 are paraphrase Masses, these latter modifications or elaborations of plainsong melodies: only 5 look back to the type of Mass with a tenor *cantus firmus* used—mainly—throughout, and only 4 are entirely free compositions. The *Missa Brevis* comes into the latter category, *Aeterna Christi munera* is a paraphrase of the plainsong hymn, *Assumpta est Maria* is a parody of the composer's motet with that title, both therefore being also paraphrases of the plain-song antiphon. The parody Mass *Hodie Christus natus est,* based on the composer's joyous Christmas motet, is one of three for antiphonal choirs and the only one that begins "with all the voices in block-chord harmony rather than imitation".

In the Masses *Assumpta est Maria* and *Lauda Sion* Palestrina quotes the opening notes of the plainsong melodies of the antiphon and Sequence on which they are respectively founded at the start of each movement (but not in the *Benedictus* or *Agnus Dei* II of the *Assumpta*). It may be remarked here that the quite frequent omission of *Agnus Dei . . . dona nobis pacem* in Palestrina's Masses is traceable to his connection with St John Lateran where then (as now) it was by long tradition not used. Pope Innocent III (1198–1216) says that in his day many churches retained "the older usage" and this was generally observed on Holy Thursday, when the station was at St John Lateran; and it is now observed once more in the restored rite of Holy Week.

For radiant beauty of sound and spiritual fervour the motet and Mass *Assumpta est Maria* are without parallel in Palestrina's work, or in that of any other composer. In the second half of the motet the short theme to the words *quae est ista quae progreditur quasi aurora* ("who is she that cometh up like the rising dawn") is used, in the Mass, whenever our Lord is personally invoked, and so at the start of *Christe eleison* (alto), *Benedictus* (soprano), etc.; and in the same way the majestic theme in the motet *cum Christo regnat in aeternum* ("Mary reigns with Christ for ever") is used with equally splendid effect at the close of *Kyrie* II, *Gloria, Credo* (*et vitam venturi saeculi*) and *Agnus Dei* II, in each case, as in the motet, being sung by the basses. In the first two sections of the motet sopranos and tenors are constantly in their upper range, being given some relief in the lower-pitched opening section of the second half. In the more extended form of the Mass Palestrina makes this contrast at *Christe eleison,* scored only for alto and tenors, and *Benedictus* (two sopranos, alto, tenor). The sudden and thrilling change of triple time at *Jubilate et exultate* ("Rejoice and exult") is paralleled in the *Hosanna* of the *Sanctus*, which sounds as if all the morning stars were dancing and singing with joy. Palestrina's contrasts of homophony and polyphony can be very well studied in this superb Mass, and also his symbolic word painting. The opening notes of the plainsong underline the meaning of the feast, but his own touches come in such passages as *descendit de coelis*, a downward phrase and the same first seven notes, again starting on high G (but this time with sopranos, not tenors, doubling) at *et homo factus est*. The four-part *Benedictus* has groups of notes of smaller value that go up and down the scale like flights of angels. This rather lengthy analysis may also serve as indicating the workings of the parody technique of the period.

Though Palestrina is certainly at his greatest in his Masses he composed motets as beautiful as those of any of his contemporaries. The well-known *Super flumina Babylonis* is a fine example of balanced phrases, rising to a high pitch of emotion (and attaining the highest musical pitch) at the second and final singing of *suspendimus organa nostra*.

As has been said before a composer is freer to use pictorial or symbolic illustration in the "tone-poem" of the motet than in the Mass—for a motet is an extra-liturgical piece. So we find Palestrina in the joyful *Exultate Deo*, illustrating the trumpet blowing up on the new moon and other instruments mentioned in the psalm, and in *Surge illuminare* vividly—as always with the word *surge*—illustrating "Rise (and shine)" in the upward flight of the notes, and writing tremendous chordal passages at *et gloria Domini super te orta est* ("and the glory of the Lord has encompassed you"). (As not infrequently happens, and not only with Palestrina, the second part of the motet is not quite up to the same standard.) *Jubilate Deo*, another but brief double-choir motet, has an enchanting *Gloria Patri* in triple time, the two choirs sharing the successive clauses of the text between them and joining to make a massive conclusion.

Nothing new can be said of the exquisite and far famed setting of *Stabat Mater* except that more often than not it is poorly—that is unimaginatively—sung, and so disappoints. But perhaps only angels could bring out the true beauty of its ending, *Paradisi gloria,* a matter of only ten bars, music that must sound what it truly is—not of this world.

St Philip of Neri, a life-long friend of Palestrina's, founded his Congregation of the Oratory "for the contemplation of celestial things by means of heavenly harmonies" (in an actual as well as a metaphorical sense). Those words may well stand for a poetic description of Palestrina's art. Baini tells us the composer died in the arms of the saint. There is no evidence to support this, but one would like to think it was so.

The idea that all later sixteenth-century church music was sung *a capella* (which has come to mean unaccompanied), that still lingers on, arose from a complete misunderstanding of the nature of the Sistine Chapel choir. This was the pope's special body of singers and quite distinct from the choirs of the Julian Chapel (St Peter's) or St John Lateran. Whatever basilica the pope attended his choir went with him and observed their tradition of singing *a capella.* Choirs of the basilicas were allowed to sing only in *Tu es Petrus* at his entrance.

The fact that soon after Palestrina's death instrumental accompaniments were added to his Masses shows what the general tendency was. Thus his pupil Felice Anerio added an instrumental *continuo* part to several of the Masses, among them the *Papae Marcelli*, and, a further "improvement", reduced the six vocal parts to four. Much later Bach added a more elaborate instrumental accompaniment to the *Kyrie* and *Gloria* of the six-part Mass *Sine nomine* and performed them at St Thomas', Leipzig.

The present writer feels that, whatever the prevailing fashion, Palestrina's music demands to be sung *a capella* and would extend the principle to most of sixteenth-century sacred polyphony. Add an instrument and the music is that much more shackled to the earth.

In conclusion one must reiterate that, from the liturgical point of view, the most perfect polyphonic music ever composed is that of Palestrina's, from the most highly organized Mass to the simplest hymn or litany setting, or the sublime *Improperia*—in which Berlioz, who should have known better, could only see "a few chords and suspensions", and on this basis dismissed Palestrina as having skill but no genius.

Marenzio, Nanino and Anerio

Mention must be made of three other Roman contemporaries of Palestrina, Luca Marenzio (1553–99), the greatest master of the madrigal, Giovanni Maria Nanino (*c.* 1543–1607) and Felice Anerio (*c.* 1564–1614). In Marenzio's excellent collection of motets there is a fine setting for double-choir of *Jubilate Deo* and the setting of *Hodie Christus natus est* with which his one publication of sacred music begins. The writing up to the cries of *Noe, noe, exultant justi* is elaborate and the composer builds up to the *Gloria in excelsis Deo* with which the words of the plainsong antiphon end, at which point he quotes very effectively the plainsong intonation of the *Gloria* in all the parts. He mutes his tendency, as a madrigal composer, to vivid word-painting but makes a poignant effect in the motet for the feast of the Holy Innocents at the words *occisi sunt* ("they were killed"). Nanino was much addicted to canon, of which he was a master, but he lays aside his learning in a beautiful setting of *Diffusa est gratia* and in a setting of *Hodie Christus natus est* in which he puts the "Noe" section into triple time on its first appearance and writes brilliant scale passages for the phrases at *canunt angeli, laetentur archangeli.* He quotes the opening notes of the plainsong antiphon in all four voices at the start of the motet.

Felice Anerio was given, as Reese says, to descriptive devices his master would not have used. In *Factum est silentium,* which has a text taken from the first responsory at Matins for the feast of St Michael the Archangel, Anerio's immediate repetitions of "the thousands of thousands and hundreds of thousands who minister to the all-powerful God", followed by a repetition of the whole of the final section of the motet, vividly underline the picture of vast hosts.

His short motet *O Jesu mi dulcissime* for three voices with its repetitions of *O spes spirantis animae* ("O hope of the aspiring soul") is most touching.

THE SPANISH SCHOOL

The Netherland and Italian composers, by the middle of the sixteenth century, had forged an international polyphonic technique which, however, could accommodate national differences of temperament, and this can be clearly seen in the music of Victoria and his immediate predecessors, two of whom will be mentioned here, Cristobal de Morales (*c.* 1500: died 1553) and his pupil Francisco Guerrero (1528–99). Both were born at Seville and both went to Rome, Morales to sing in the papal chapel, Guerrero on a visit.

Morales and Guerrero

Morales especially favoured Gregorian melodies in his Masses, which include a fine Requiem for five voices and a setting of the Office of the Dead in which plainsong alternates with polyphony. It cannot compare with Victoria's great setting. Among his motets *Emendemus in melius* stands out for grim and dramatic power. The text is that of the responsory of Ash Wednesday beginning, "Amend our lives, thoughtless sinners that we are, or the day of death may come upon

us suddenly, asking for time to repent in, and asking in vain",
and the composer introduces into the alto part the words
spoken at the imposition of the ashes, *Memento, homo, quid
pulvis, es et in pulverem reverteris* ("Remember man that
thou art dust and to dust thou shalt return"), repeating always
the second half of the sentence. This sombre "burden" is sung
six times.

Guerrero has been called "Mary's singer" and his devotion
to our Lady sweetens his music. Reese says that "both by
training and scene of activity, Guerrero was a more completely
Spanish composer than either Morales or Victoria. His five-
part *Ave virgo sanctissima* is a compilation of plainsong
Marian melodies, quoting, among others, the hymn *Ave maris
stella* and the antiphon *Salve Regina,* while in his *Missa de
beata Virgine* "there are—following an old Seville custom—
textual insertions that introduce the name of Mary into all
three sections of the *Kyrie*". There is said to be none of the
terror that comes into Morales' Requiem in Guerrero's two
Masses for the Dead.

Victoria

Tomás Luis de Victoria was born in or near Avila in 1548
and died in 1611 and it is tempting to think that he knew
St Teresa of Avila (1515–82), St John of the Cross (1543–91)
and El Greco (1547–1614). He is rarely discussed without
reference to the great visionary painter but the comparison
does not take us very far. It is true that, to make any sense of
it, one needs to hear his greatest work, the Office for Holy
Week, sung with the fervour of a Spanish choir. He wrote no
secular music and only one Mass on a secular song and one
feels that he was a priest not only in name but in every fibre
of his being.

He may have studied under Palestrina during his early
years in Rome—he went there as a boy of seventeen—and
certainly always held the Roman master in the greatest rever-

ence and was influenced musically by him. In 1571 he succeeded Palestrina as *Maestro di capella* at the Collegium Romanum and two years later went to a similar post at the Collegium Germanicum, a seminary founded by Ignatius Loyola to combat Lutheranism. In 1578 he became a resident priest at the church of San Girolamo dell Carita, where St Philip of Neri, in 1554, had instituted his Oratory, founding twenty-one years later the Congregation of the Oratory, with its headquarters at the Chiesa Nuova.

The dedication of Victoria's collection of motets and psalms published in 1583 is addressed to "the blessed Virgin Mother of God and to all the saints reigning in heavenly felicity with Christ, to celebrate their praises on occasion of their festivals and to animate with greater sweetness the devotion of the faithful". He describes himself here for the first time as a priest and declares, in the book of Masses dedicated to Philip II and also published this same year, that he had been led by a secret natural impulse to devote himself exclusively to the composition of church music, going on to say that he was now weary and wished to give his mind more to the divine contemplation befitting a priest. He fortunately retracted this apparent farewell to music and two years later published his greatest work, the Office of Holy Week. The use of a Spanish melody for the hymns *Pange lingua* and *Vexilla Regis* may indicate that he composed the settings for use in Spain or the Spanish churches in Rome.

In 1594 Victoria left Spain and took a modest post as chaplain to the convent of the Royal Discalced Carmelites at Madrid, where the daughter of the Empress Maria was a professed nun. He paid tribute to the memory of the empress, who died in 1603, with his superb *Officium Defunctorum* for six voices, which he dedicated to her daughter. Five years later, as far as can be ascertained, he died in Madrid.

It is sad that since the reconstituted liturgy of Holy Week *Tenebrae* is no longer sung in the evenings. In the great days when Richard Terry was Master of the Music at Westminster Cathedral huge crowds came to hear the magnificent singing of the choir in Victoria's (and some years, Ingegneri's) settings of the responsories; and few who were there will ever forget the solemn scene as the candles on the triangular candlestick were extinguished one by one as each psalm was ended until, after the *Benedictus,* the *Miserere* was sung in the darkness, the clergy speaking the even verses, *sotto voce,* the choir responding with the odd ones in simple polyphony. The setting brought out to the full the spiritual intensity and dramatic fervour of Victoria's music, the poignancy of the unforgettable *O vos omnes* and *Tenebrae factae sunt.*

Among the motets must be mentioned the wonderful setting of *O magnum mysterium* (the subject of one of Victoria's parody Masses) with its endearing picture of the animals being privileged to be present at the birth of Christ, the lovely *Ave Maria,* a paraphrase of the plainsong melody and preceded by its intonation. The two chordal phrases, in triple time, each echoing the other, are filled with mystical fervour. In the four-part *Duo Seraphim* Victoria—as Monteverdi was to do in his Vespers—illustrates literally "There are three that bear witness in heaven, the Father, the Son and the Holy Ghost, and these three are one", by writing the section in three parts and ending on a unison. *O quam gloriosum est regnum,* one of the finest of the Masses, has a very simple but lovely setting of *et incarnatus est* in the *Credo* with expressive pauses, and these are also found in the equally fine Mass *Quarti Toni.* In the Mass *Ave maris stella,* based on the plainsong hymn melody, the tenor sings the words of the hymn in the first *Hosanna* of the *Sanctus* and in the second *Agnus* for five voices, and the second tenor sings the melody throughout to the words of the *Agnus.* A curiosity in Victoria's works in the Mass *Pro victoria* which combines a conservative style with fanfare-like passages based on Jannequin's battle piece *La Guerre.*

LASSUS

Roland de Lassus was born *c.* 1532 at or near Mons (Hainault), a Fleming by birth, a cosmopolitan by the circumstances of his career. The beauty of his treble voice caused him to be abducted three times—fortunately for him before the age of the *castrati*—and after his youthful years in Italy he soon became famous, with publishers competing eagerly for his works. Lassus was a tireless traveller throughout Europe and his restlessness and fundamentally melancholy temperament is reflected in his music, in spite of the humour (sometimes bawdy) and liveliness of his large output of Italian, French and German secular music. He was able to write in every current style and covered a wider field of expression and experience than any of his great contemporaries. Madrigals in the Italian manner, chansons in the French manner, lieder in the German manner poured from his pen, as did motets and Masses that reflect the styles of Josquin, Palestrina and Andrea Gabrielli. His vocal lines are frequently rough and without the balance and serenity of Josquin's or Palestrina's. In emotional fervour he stands nearest to Victoria. His acute feeling for words and use of the greater licence of madrigalian technique in the motet produce many striking results. Thus the motet *Videntes stellam,* a picture of the journey and adoration of the Magi, begins with the voices, in turn, rising directly a fifth to an octave (G–D–G), as if depicting the Magi gazing up at the star. In *Dixi ergo,* the section of the motet which has a text on the vanity of earthly joys, taken from Ecclesiasticus, he gives a vivid expression to such words as *vanitas, risus, error, stultitia,* with constant changes of rhythm and divisions of voices. Charles van den Borren likens his uncouth phrases to *stultitia* to Beckmesser's absurd *vocalisés* in Wagner's *Die Meistersinger.* Lassus, of course, employed double-choir writing as, for example, in a motet *In convertendo* remarkable for its harmonies.

Lassus did not often have recourse to Gregorian chant themes but his beautiful *Salve Regina* has the plainsong melody, little altered, in the bass part. His greatest church works are not to be found in his motets or Masses (the latter, mostly in parody style, are said to be often disappointing, perhaps because his imagination needed to be fired by variety of text) but in the *Nine Lamentations of the Prophet Jeremiah*, the *Lessons from Job*, and the *Seven Penitential Psalms*. In the last section of the "First Lamentation of the Third Day" with the words "Jerusalem turn again to the Lord thy God" the sopranos leap an octave to a top G on "Jerusalem" with most poignant effect. These fine Lamentations should be better known. The *Seven Penitential Psalms* were composed at the request of Duke Albert V of Munich. Lassus had been a singer for some years in his chapel before being appointed *Kapellmeister* in 1563. The task took him the same number of years as the number of the psalms, 1563–70. The duke honoured the composer by having the work "beautifully transcribed on parchment and adorned with miniatures by his court painter Hans Mülich and then handsomely bound in two volumes in red morocco with silver clasps". It was printed in 1584. Samuel Quicekelberg, a physician to the duke's court, describing these miniatures, says of the music:

> He expressed (the content) so aptly with lamenting and plaintive melody, adapting where it was necessary (the music) to the subject and the words, expressing the power of the different emotions, presenting the subject as if acted before the eyes, that one cannot know whether the sweetness of the emotions more adorns the plaintive melodies or the plaintive melodies the sweetness of the emotions. This kind of music they call *musica reservata*.[2]

The definition is valuable. *Musica reservata* was composed, as a theorist of the time writes, "for trained ears at private entertainment of lords and princes", and we must therefore

[2] *Music in the Renaissance*, p. 513.

assume that the *Penitential Psalms* were not sung in church. They are written mainly for five voices, with sections for duets, trios and quartets and with the use of a psalm tone (No. 6) only in De profundis. This was perhaps sung *a capella*, but instrumental accompaniment would have been used in the rest of the psalms.

JACOB HANDL

This composer is also known by his Latin name Gallus, owing to the fact that his name may originally have been Peterlin (cock) in Slovenian. He was born in Rybnica Caniola (now in Jugoslavia) and died at Prague in 1591. Most of his works were written in Bohemia and Moravia. His motet *Mirabile mysterium*, one of a collection of motets for the whole of the liturgical year published as *Opus Musicum*, in four books, between 1586 and 1591, is well known for its chromaticisms. In complete contrast is the wholly chordal and diatonic motet *Ecce, quomodo moritur justus*: but his most attractive motets are those that end with dance-like Alleluias, betokening a great cheerfulness of spirit. Among these are the double-choir motets *Repleti sunt omnes* and *Hac dies confirma hoc Deus* for four voices. He often writes squarely, in the German manner, but conversely shows a desire to be free of rhythmical chains. Thus in the second part of the motet *Ecce concipies* he uses within the space of sixteen bars 3/4, 2/4, 3/4, 2/4, 4/4 (according to the modern transcription). Handl cannot be neatly docketed, and that is one of his attractions.

THE ENGLISH SCHOOL: TAVERNER, TYE, TALLIS, BYRD

John Taverner is the oldest of the great quartet of English composers named above. He was born *c.* 1495 and appears to have been a native of Tattershall (or Boston) where he became a boy chorister at the collegiate church founded by Sir Ralph Cromwell in 1439. In 1525–6 he was appointed the first master of the music of Cardinal Wolsey's College, Oxford (now Christ Church), escaping imprisonment for having, with others, disseminated heretical books, on the grounds that "he was but a musician". Taverner resigned from his post in 1530 and after the final break between the papacy and England in 1534 he turned informer—having secured a lucrative appointment from Thomas Cromwell—and took part enthusiastically in the suppression of the monasteries, securing possession of two friaries at Boston for himself. He died *c.* 1548.

This far from admirable character is reported to have said that "he repented him very muche that he had made songes to Popish ditties in the tyme of his blindness", these "songs" being his motets and so not including his famous Mass on the secular tune *The Westron Wynde*, the original of which is unknown but which, as H. B. Collins says in the preface to his edition of the Mass, "is redolent of the English countryside". The melody remains almost unchanged throughout being placed in each of the voices except the alto, the other parts consisting of variations on it. Each movement has the melody in the treble part at the start. As there is no *Kyrie*, Mr Collins has adapted the *Benedictus* for the purpose and filled in the omitted clauses of the *Credo* with the appropriate plainsong phrases from *Credo* I.

The well-defined tune is always kept to the fore and the masterly counterpoint moves so freely about it that the Mass, composed not later than 1530, makes an immediate, even a popular appeal and can be considered technically more original than any Mass that had yet appeared abroad. It was in Taverner's Mass *Gloria tibi Trinitas* based on the first antiphon at Lauds of the feast of the Holy Trinity that the clue was found for the innumerable instrumental pieces based on the antiphon but given a title, *In nomine*, which is not in the text. The clue lies in Taverner's *Benedictus* (*qui venit* in nomine *Domini*) in which he quotes the whole of the antiphon melody.

Christopher Tye's "Westron Wynde" Mass, which has the tune throughout in the one voice, the alto, in which it does not appear in Taverner's Mass on the same melody, is almost as fine a work as its predecessor and there are two motets, strongly contrasted in subject, that must be mentioned, the five-part *Miserere mei Deus*, beginning sombrely but touchingly brightening at the words "For in thee my soul takes refuge", and the exultant *Omnes gentes plaudite manibus*.

Tye seems to have been a man of character, for once when Queen Elizabeth sent him a message to say he was "out of tune" he sent back word that "it was her Majesty's ears that were out of tune". A bold reply.

Thomas Tallis, organist of Waltham Abbey until the dissolution of the monastery in 1540, under Henry VIII, became soon afterwards a Gentleman of the Chapel Royal and so remained under Edward VI and Mary and Elizabeth up to his death in 1585. His canon hymn tune "Glory to Thee, my God, this night" is universally known and so, among concertgoers, because of Vaughan Williams' splendid *Tallis Fantasia*, is the tune taken from nine composed for Archbishop Parker's Psalter. Among his motets is a beautiful setting of *In jejunio et fletu* for Lent but his greatest work is the *Lamentations of the Prophet Jeremiah* (also finely set by Tye's son-in-law Robert White) with its unforgettable and sorrowful burden *Jerusalem convertere ad Dominum Deum tuum*. What magnificent music the *Lamentations* called forth in the sixteenth century! Tallis's settings of Office hymns, the odd verses, with a few exceptions, left in plainsong, the even set to four-part polyphony, are very beautiful. *Salvator mundi* has the melody of *Veni creator Spiritus*. Finally there is his famous forty-part motet *Spem in alium non habui*. Thomas Tudway (*c*. 1650–1726), Professor of Music in Cambridge University, considered that this motet was to be taken as a memorial of Tallis's immense contrapuntal skill, whereas we know it is most effective in performance, having a splendour of sound that makes it the equal of any such large-scale works by Josquin, Okeghem or the later Venetians.

Thomas Morley, Byrd's most famous pupil, spoke of his master in the course of his *Plaine and Easie Introduction to Musicke* as a man "never without reverence to be named of the musicians", a moving tribute echoed by all the English musicians of his day and also by many abroad where "his skill doth shyne". Nearly 300 years after Byrd's death, in 1623, Richard Terry, then a young music master at Downside Abbey, gave, with his choir at Ealing Priory, the first performance since the Reformation, or perhaps ever, of Byrd's great five-part Mass, which he scored, as so much else, from the original part books, but had to have published by a German firm, the English firms taking no interest in it at all. Comparing it with the music of Palestrina, Terry wrote: "As a powerful conception of fitting music to hymn the glory of the Eternal Trinity Byrd's *Sanctus* is not inferior even to the *Sanctus* of *Missa Papae Marcelli* that 'sound of many waters'. . . . Palestrina himself never wrote anything more tenderly beautiful, more serene and peaceful than the *Agnus Dei,* as it rises from flight to flight of calm ecstasy."

Now that the glories of Tudor music, neglected for so long, have been revealed by the labours of Terry, Dr E. H. Fellowes, Charles Kennedy Scott, Denis Stevens and others, we know how true this is. It became possible to speak of Byrd in the same breath as his contemporaries, Lassus, Palestrina and Victoria: and he not only belongs to that glorious company but shows himself as the most versatile of them all. In addition to his Roman and Anglican church music, his madrigals and solo songs, he composed also a wealth of keyboard music and some chamber music, including the five-part *Fantasia* for strings.

Byrd, born *c.* 1542, was only six when the Act of Uniformity was passed and so he spent the whole of his professional life, from his appointment as organist of Lincoln Cathedral, in 1563, to his long service as organist of the Chapel Royal, in the service of the Anglican Church. He expressed a wish in his will "to live and die a true and perfect member of God's holy Catholic Church", which he was. Elizabeth had the wit to recognize in him a genius of the highest order, a "stiff Papist" indeed, but a loyal subject and he was never seriously interfered with in the practice of his religion. In 1575 Elizabeth granted Tallis, whose pupil he had been, and Byrd licence to print "songe or songes in partes for Churche or chamber", in any language, the outcome of which was a set of *Cantiones Sacrae* with words chosen so as to give no offence to the Queen. It was a different matter with the *Gradualia,* published in 1605 and 1607 (after Tallis's death) and quite openly designed for use in the Roman Church with texts devoted to our Lady, the Saints and the Blessed Sacrament.

Byrd explained his point of view in composing church music. "There is a certain hidden power, as I learnt by experience, in the thoughts underlying the words themselves: so that, as one meditates on the sacred words and constantly and seriously considers them, the right notes, in some unexplicable manner, suggest themselves quite spontaneously."

Byrd rarely uses plainsong melodies but in his polyphonic setting of the hymn *Christe qui lux es et dies* he gives the plainsong to each of the five voices in turn, from the lowest to the highest part, with lovely effect. Among his many fine motets must be mentioned *Justorum animae* for feasts of Many Martyrs. The words *in pace* passing from voice to voice have a celestial beauty (lacking in Lassus's setting of the same words) that is only equalled in the *dona nobis pacem* sections of the three Masses. In each of these, incidentally, Byrd sets the *Kyrie*: and that of the three-part Mass, a marvel of simplicity and art, is far from being "dull", as one commentator has said.

Byrd can never have heard any of his Latin church music performed and it is intensely moving to find him adding to his exquisite, and unsurpassed, setting of *Ave verum* the petition *miserere mei*. The present author has searched for any parallel to this exceptional use of the personal pronoun and found it only in a setting by Peter Phillips, then living abroad, who had probably come to know of Byrd's motet.

Both Peter Phillips (*c*. 1560–1633) and Richard Deering († *c*. 1630) spent most of their lives abroad and made notable additions to church music. Deering's dramatic *Vox in Rama* and Christmas motet *Quem vidistis pastores* are outstanding. The latter has a joyful outburst of Alleluias at the close. Phillips' *Alma Redemptoris Mater* and the dramatic *Surge Petre* (the angel's command in delivering the apostle from the prison) are equally fine. The last word, in this section, must again refer to the great years of Richard Terry's service at Westminster Cathedral. The range of sixteenth-century music he presented there—as one can read in Hilda Andrews' biography—is quite extraordinary and nothing like it has been heard since. Cardinal Vaughan, to whom Terry was devoted, had the vision to see what could be done, and was done. This was denied in anything like the same measure to his successors. Vaughan provided him with an assistant organist and choirmaster and *fourteen* men, in addition to the boys, for the daily services. In 1912 the fourteen had been reduced to nine: and today one may see only four, or even a less number of men, come down from the retro-choir after Mass.

THE VENETIAN SCHOOL

Venice seems to have been a musical city ever since its founders came from Aquileia, whose musicians were praised by Jerome in 379. Pride in the State grew with its increasing power and fame and the saying "we are first of all Venetians and then Christians" might stand as the motto of the ceremonial compositions that became one of its great glories. There were numerous academies of music and it was in Venice that Petrucci, in 1498, established the first music publishing house. If we needed further evidence of the musicality of the city it can be seen in well-known paintings by Giorgione, Titian, Tintoretto and Veronese. The latter introduces into his *Wedding Feast at Cana* portraits of himself, Titian, Tintoretto and Bassano all playing musical instruments.

Every visitor to St Mark's has the *cori spezzati* pointed out to him, the two choir-organ galleries which gave composers from the end of the fifteenth century opportunity for the polychoral writing which Giovanni Gabrielli was to bring to its highest peak of perfection. The concept of antiphonal singing, one group of singers (or even single individuals) responding to another, is as old as music itself and is, of course, found in a developed form in Gregorian chant and the polyphonic periods we have been discussing. Cecil Gray in his *History of Music* fancifully points out that the characteristic structural features of the city are reproduced in the polychoral writing of the Venetian composers. "The city is constructed like a six-part double-choir . . . and the Grand Canal itself is like an antiphon in which one group of palaces on one side replies to one group on the other, like choir to choir, until they finally unite in the majestic full close of the Piazza di San Marco."

Willaert and the Gabriellis

When Adrian Willaert, who had been a pupil of Jean Monton, was appointed *Maestro di capella* at St Mark's in 1527 and introduced Flemish polyphony there, he found the tradition of double-choir writing active and adopted it in his psalm settings. For this purpose he carefully studied problems of balance and sonority, but he does not entirely eschew counterpoint. His style of writing, however, influenced Lassus and Palestrina among others outside Venice, and his use of it for brilliant ceremonial occasions—for example in praise of the Duke of Bavaria—in turn influenced his pupil Andrea Gabrielli (*c.* 1510–86), uncle of Giovanni Gabrielli (1557–1617), both of whom became famous organists and masters of the music of St Mark's.

Andrea Gabrielli brought to his polychoral motets the rapid exchanges and overlappings between the choirs, their uniting in sonorous *tutti*, and the fundamentally simple harmonic texture demanded by the circumstances. When his polychoral works were published by his nephew in 1587 they were called *Concerti* and the term is significant of a change in outlook. From now on the use of *cori spezzati* in Venice became general. In the music of Giovanni Gabrielli, its greatest master, this kind of writing attains its greatest glory. He was able to take full advantage of the invention of a notation for *continuo* playing and in his *Sacrae Symphoniae* (1597) he undoubtedly made use of instruments. In the later and posthumously printed collection with the same title there is a marked difference of style between soloists, who are given virtuoso parts, and tutti, there are orchestral interludes of a dance-like character, clearly defined sections, solo, duet, trio, orchestral, and a climax is achieved with all available forces. This is truly music of the early baroque, Counter-Reformation music, according to Jesuit notions.

Gabrielli's motet *In ecclesiis* for double choir, one of soloists, one of chorus, instruments and organ, is fairly well known. The instruments are specified, three cornetti, violino (viola) and two trombones. When all the forces join together at *Deus adjutor noster* there are some astonishing chromatic progressions that show how much more inventive Giovanni was than his uncle. Even finer is *O Domine Jesu Christe* in which a choir of four voices (alto, two tenors and bass) is responded to by one of higher voices (two sopranos, alto, baritone) succeeding to the other almost imperceptibly, the sounds growing ever more radiant, the close full of ecstatic joy. One is reminded of the strong contrasts of light and colour in the pictures of Correggio.

It is worth remarking here that the Roman school of church music became somewhat infected by baroque architecture of the kind seen in Vignola's Church of the Gesù and it was a Roman master, Orazio Benevoli, who composed the huge festival Mass in the polychoral style for the inauguration of the new cathedral in Salzburg in 1628. The score requires fifty-three staves on each page and the whole structure is held together by a *basso continuo* consisting of all the bass instruments (strings and wind), two organs, harpsichord (hardly audible surely) and so on. As a writer on the work says, "it is as if Bernini's Spanish staircase and his gigantic colonnades before St Peter's had been transformed into music". The use of an independent *basso continuo*, that is one that did not merely double the vocal bass part, signalized the end of the great polyphonic period. It was no longer a question of the top part being first among equals (even if that) but of a new polarity between top part and bass, allowing the former far greater freedom of embellishment and expression. Writing for *cori spezzati* came to an end about 1625 when new ways of obtaining contrasts were developed. The ideals of the Venetian school we have been discussing were very different from those of the great Roman school, who used double-choir writing, however influenced by Venice, in a manner more befitting the liturgy; but also the brilliance and varied colour of the Venetian style makes a tremendous impact on the listener and in its own way, is a great contribution to sacred music.

CHAPTER VIII

SOLO, CHORUS AND ORCHESTRA: SEVENTEENTH TO NINETEENTH CENTURIES

MONTEVERDI

Claudio Monteverdi, who was born at Cremona in 1567, studied under Ingegneri, became violist and singer in the court and chapel of the Duke of Mantua and master of the choir in 1601, was appointed to a similar position at St Mark's, Venice, in 1613, and remained there until his death in 1643. He was ordained priest in 1632. The engraved portrait of him, published in Venice in 1644, is that of a deeply thoughtful man who had, as we know, experienced many trials and tribulations. Ten years after his death interest in this great composer, who had been famous and honoured throughout Europe, began to fade and it was not until Malipiero's edition of the complete works—three large volumes of which are devoted to his church music—became available, between 1926 and 1942, that musicians were able to assess the full stature of his genius, and that the revival of interest in him in our time, begun with the first modern reprint of *Orfeo*, continued on a large scale.

In 1610, and therefore while still at Mantua, Monteverdi put together a six-part Mass and a setting of Vespers of our Lady as a collection to impress Pope Paul V, to whom they are dedicated, and even more the Chapter of St Mark's. Monteverdi had been dismissed by Duke Francis IV Gonzaga, successor to Vincenzo I, and the death of G. C. Martinengo, master of the chapel of St Mark's on July 19th, 1613, made him eager to secure the most coveted position in Europe. He was unanimously elected a month later. Monteverdi is a pivotal figure. He declared that "the modern composer builds on the foundation of truth" and in his church music that meant for him writing in two styles which he called the First and the Second Practices. The former was the style roughly described as Palestrinian and is beautifully displayed in his six-part Mass on motifs taken from a motet, *In illo tempore,* by the Flemish composer Nicolas Gombert. It is, therefore, a late example of the parody Mass: but Monteverdi pays tribute to the comparatively recent introduction of a *basso continuo* for organ. The Vespers is the supreme example of his Second Practice, the logical outcome of the experience of a century and of the prevailing techniques, in its solo passages, of vocal writing. It is significant that in the first number, *Domine ad adjuvandum me festina* (the choral response to the priest's intoning of the versicle *Deus in adjutorium meum intende*) Monteverdi uses, in the orchestral accompaniment, the *Toccata* for brass with which his *Orfeo* begins, while the six voices recite the words rhythmically on one note, except for the closing cadence. Here is the *stile concitato*, the "agitated" or dramatic style that Monteverdi brought to perfection in his *Eighth Book of Madrigals* published in 1638.

The first performance of the *Vespers* in England, which took place in London in 1946, made a tremendous impression and there are now at least five editions of the work available, reflecting the various views of their editors as to what instruments or voices should be used where the composer has left the question open. Professor Denis Stevens[1] was alone in making it clear that Monteverdi never meant the *Vespers* to be sung through, one number after another, as they were first printed and as printed later in the Malipiero edition. As it stands the *Vespers* is not a liturgical work. The five antiphons for solo voices or groups of soloists, with chorus also participating in two of them, are motets, and the text of one of them, *Duo Seraphim* (a responsory from Matins on the Feast of the Most Holy Trinity), has no relation to our Lady at all, while all the motets are lengthy and in no sense antiphons for the psalms. The psalms, the hymn *Ave maris stella* and *Magnificat* (of which there are two versions, the second one being of a simpler character) form a symmetrical group, with constant quoting of psalm tones and the canticle tone in the psalms and *Magnificat* and the plainsong melody in the hymn. The interpolated *Sonata sopra Sancta Maria* could have no part in *Vespers*. In it the chorus, in unison, sing the words *Sancta Maria, ora pro nobis,* on the plainsong melody from The Litany of Loreto, to an instrumental part with constant changes of figuration, and often of a trivial character.

Of the two other Masses extant by Monteverdi, both are in four parts and both in the manner of the First Practice. The one published in 1641, three years before his death, is a fine and beautiful work and—strangely according to our notions of style—provides for alternative versions of *Crucifixus, Et resurrexit* and *Et iterum venturi saeculi* in the *concertante* style, that is with chromatic writing and instrumentation in the manner of the *Vespers*. The large volumes of his sacred music include psalms and hymn settings in this style, motets, and solo motets in both styles.

There is much lovely and striking music in these works: and one cannot fail to admire those in the "modern style" even while hearing the death-knell of the great ages of liturgical church music. The means Monteverdi so often uses

---

[1] Denis Stevens, *Vespers by Claudio Monteverdi*, edited from the original publication of 1610, Novello, 1961.

are really those of the theatre: and this note will be sounded
thereafter in no uncertain manner in the "Viennese" Masses.
Monteverdi's use of echo effects in the *Vespers* bears no
relation, of course, to the resources offered by St Mark's, the
double-choir writing of the kind associated with the Gabriellis
and the Venetian School of the sixteenth century, which was
already out of fashion in his time.

FRENCH CHURCH MUSIC

The polyphonic style gave place very slowly in France to
the *stile nuovo* of Monteverdi, his contemporaries and immediate successors, but some of the works of one composer,
Henri du Mont (1610–84), are still sung in France today. One
finds in parish manuals his plainsong Masses, and his small
motets for one to three voices, with organ accompaniment, are
simple and useful material for choirs of moderate accomplishment. The baroque style reached its climax in the reign of
Louis XIV (1643–1715) the *Roi Soleil,* and because the king
preferred low Mass to the more lengthy high Mass, composers
sought to dignify the occasion by introducing motets, often
with elaborate instrumental accompaniment, into the service.
Some of these motets, in which Jean-Baptiste Lully (1632–87)
excelled, were in fact cantatas for soloists, chorus and orchestra; others, such as Lully's *Elévations* for one or two voices
and *basso continuo,* were simpler and intimate in style as
befitting the occasion. Lully's vast *Te Deum,* with its trumpets
and drums, is well known and speaks of the ceremonial
splendour that appealed to the congregations of the time. The
secular spirit had triumphed: and Mass and Vespers were apt
to be social occasions enlivened by concerts. They were, no
doubt, good concerts and not without piety and fervour: but
it is a relief to turn from Lully's arid style, in his big works,
to the church music of Marc Antoine Charpentier (1634–1704),
who had studied with Carissimi and acquired the gracious,

melodic Italian style which the Italian-born Lully, who left Italy for France when he was fourteen, had hardly known. Charpentier, who became master of music at the Sainte-Chapelle, Paris, and had a large choir at his disposal, composed over 500 sacred works, oratorios, motets, *Te Deums* and Masses. Among the latter is the delightful Christmas *Messe de Minuit*, in which each movement is based on an old French carol.

"On the whole," Henri Prunières writes in his *New History of Music*, "French religious music of this period is admittedly superficial; but there are nevertheless occasions when one can admire its power, pathos and imagination." The last two qualities are prominent in the *Leçons de Ténèbres* for Good Friday of François Couperin (1668–1733). The three of these extant, out of the six he composed, were written for an unknown community of nuns; the first two are set for one voice, the third for two, with organ accompaniment, to which, the composer says, viola or violin may be added. The third *Leçon* rises to a high emotional pitch at the closing words *Jerusalem, Jerusalem, convertere ad Dominum Deum tuum*. Among the motets for one voice is one remarkable for declamatory power *Quid retribuam Domino*, while the florid and expansive style of the time is well exemplified in the Easter motet for two voices and continuo, *Haec est dies*, preceded by joyful cries of "Victoria". There should also be mentioned the charming *Motet de Sainte-Suzanne*.

THE "VIENNESE MASSES"

The instrumental Mass of the Neapolitan school of Alessandro Scarlatti, with its classic tonality and operatic style, passed naturally as orchestral resources and compositional technique developed into the orchestral Mass and that, in the Masses of Haydn, Mozart, and above all Beethoven, into the symphonic Mass. The principle of the *concerto grosso* with its

contrasts of *tutti* and solo sections in the various sections of
the Ordinary of the Mass was adopted and the principle of the
cantata in which the text within each movement of the Ordinary is split up into sections for solo or for chorus, and so
forth. We have seen in the Mass settings described in previous
portions of this book that contrast was arrived at in reducing
the number of voices, let us say, in the *Benedictus* of the
Sanctus, and at other points: and the seeds of such contrast go
back to the singing of the psalms in the synagogue. The development is a logical one, but it was powerfully influenced by
the harmonic revolution of the seventeenth century, and above
all by the birth of opera and concentration on other forms of
secular music. To say that just as composers in the past had
drawn on secular musical themes in their sacred music, chan-
son, canzone, madrigal, etc., so eighteenth-century composers
drew on opera or serenade, is to simplify the position unduly:
for the secular elements had previously been transformed in
such a manner as to be unrecognizable, they acquired a new
ethos. This is not the case with the so-called Viennese Masses.

Discussion of this matter usually generates more heat than
light and no good is done by looking at it from the point of
view of the *Motu proprio* of Pius X until the historical
position is understood.

Haydn and Mozart—for one must deal here only with such
outstanding figures—naturally wrote in the language of their
time; they wrote much beautiful and moving music informed
by sincere piety: but they wrote at a time when Joseph II, the
"emperor-sacristan", was engaged in reforming the liturgy
according to his own ideas, and when Enlightenment and
Absolutism were both at work. It is a comment on the cynical
outlook of some high ecclesiastics that Mozart's detested
Archbishop of Salzburg should have hung on the walls of his
study portraits of Voltaire and Rousseau! It is true that
Leopold II, after the death of Joseph in 1790, restored the old
order, but much damage had been done. Polytextuality revives

in the *Missa Brevis* settings of *Gloria* and *Credo* of the time, and verbal repetition is constant, as for example in the *Et incarnatus est* section of Haydn's B flat Mass (*Heiligemesse*). This repetitiveness becomes most tiresome in the *Benedictus* of the *Sanctus*, often given to a solo quartet who, to entertain the congregation, filled up the silent space between the consecration and the *Pater Noster*. Plainsong was ignored to the extent that, at Salzburg, Mozart composed his so-called "Epistle" sonatas for strings and organ to be played between Epistle and Gospel, instead of the singing of the plainsong Gradual and Alleluia. The personal point of view obtrudes. Haydn once said he could set *qui tollis peccata mundi* in *Agnus Dei* joyfully because he thought not of the sins so much as the taking away of them—a charming presumption. No doubt he and Mozart were often activated by the true spirit of the liturgical text, but even more by musical reasons. Few, if any, commentators have taken note of the fact that in his sensuously beautiful *Ave Verum* Mozart, reproducing at the climax phrases from the "writing" quintet in Act 1 of *Così fan tutte*, ends at the words *in examine*, cutting out entirely the exquisite words at the close, *O Jesu dulcis, O Jesu pie, O Jesu fili Mariae*, the real climax of the prayer. How different from Byrd's earnest dwelling on the text "so that the right notes spontaneously suggest themselves". But writers who champion the Haydn and Mozart Masses seem either indifferent to, or ignorant of, what the Mass really stands for. This brings us to the crucial point. Nicolas Powell, in a very sympathetic and appealing book *From Baroque to Rococo*, makes a strong case for the kind of church architecture known to Haydn and Mozart. He writes: "It is the mirror of heaven—of the unattainable to which so many still aspire. Never in the history of modern art was there a more happily conceived intention. Never were the essence of belief and its outward signs more brilliantly portrayed." Brilliantly, yes; prayerfully, no.

The opposing point of view is put by Father Joseph Jungmann, S.J., in his monumental book on *The Mass of the Roman Rite*, and can only here be briefly summarized.

Music spread its gorgeous mantle over the whole Mass, so that the other details of the rite had scarcely any significance. Encouraged by the moderate attitude of the Council of Trent, it had developed into mighty proportions. . . . The victorious temper of the post-Tridentine age . . . found its triumphal voice in this music. It is significant that the princely courts, both great and small, were the first places where this type of church music was cultivated and where it reached its splendour . . . the liturgy was not only submerged under this ever-growing art but actually suppressed, so that even at this time there were festive occasions which might best be described as "church concerts with liturgical accompaniment." . . . Looking at the Host at the consecration no longer possessed the attraction and significance that it had . . . the new age sought not the sight of the holy, but the beautiful in art and universe. And so the church became a great hall, its walls shimmering with marble and gold.[2]

One need only look at the many photographs of the interior of the baroque and rococo churches of Germany and Austria to see how diminished the altar is by the massive decoration above it and how restless and unprayerful the whole effect is.

The whole matter is summed up in Mozart's greatest but unfinished Mass, the C minor, K.427. There is wonderful music in the *Gratias* and above all in the *Qui tollis,* for double chorus, of the *Gloria*: but the intervening duet for two sopranos, *Domine Deus*, and the trio (with the two sopranos joined by a tenor) *Quoniam tu solus sanctus* are quite unworthy of them.

The soprano solo *Et incarnatus est* with three obbligato wind instruments was written to display the vocal talent of Mozart's wife and has a cadenza for all concerned on the syllable *fac-*

[2] Joseph A. Jungmann, S.J., *The Mass of the Roman Rite* (*Missarum Sollemnia*) (New York, Benziger, 1951; London, Burns & Oates, 1957), I, p. 148.

of *factus est*. This is lovely music, but as artificial as any coloratura aria in an opera, and as little defensible in the Mass.

To say that in Mozart's Masses "the image of Christ appears, pure and beautiful as only the early Christians could see him" may be taken as fairly true as related to the Apollo-like figure found in the mosaics of the fifth century, but seems to the present author a very extraordinary statement.[3]

One is, quite frankly, ravished by the beauty of the soprano solo, with male chorus, *Laudate Dominum* from the *Vesperae Solemnes de Confessore* (K.339) and by many other things in Mozart's sacred music, and also in Haydn's: but one is not converted to the point of view of their apologists, especially in the Masses. They may be, like the baroque churches, an expression of Austrian piety and that must be respected: they are not an expression of what the Universal Church asks of her composers.

BEETHOVEN AND SCHUBERT

It is startling to find Beethoven described, in the chapter on "Bruckner as Church Composer" from a book, *Bruckner, Mahler and Schoenberg* by Dika Newlin (published in 1947), as follows: "the great ecclesiastical works of . . . Protestant composers (Bach, Beethoven) or Catholics (Bruckner, Liszt)", and it is wearying to come across, over and over again, such statements as that Beethoven studied the text of the Mass "free from any dogmatic intermediation between himself and his Maker". The writers who express themselves in this muddled fashion would be hard put to define "dogmatic intermediation".

Beethoven said of his beautiful C major Mass, composed for liturgical use, in 1807, at the request of Prince Esterhazy,

[3] There are several of Mozart's short Masses perfectly suited to liturgical use, for example those in F (K. 192), D (K. 194) and C (K. 257).

that "he had treated the text as it has seldom been treated". That is the simple truth. The words, with many composers, had long been an excuse for music rather than an expression of what lay behind them. Beethoven sought out the meaning of the familiar words of the Ordinary and, in the *Credo,* of the dogmatic truths there to be found: and in the *Missa Solemnis* of 1818–23 he went even more seriously into the matter, having the Latin translated into German so that he could meditate on the implications of the words even more deeply than before. This great work declares unequivocally "This is what I believe—here is the nature of my relation to God": and no one with any understanding of what is involved could doubt that the result is a profoundly Catholic work. The Mass was intended for a big ceremonial occasion, the enthronement of Beethoven's pupil and friend, Archduke Rudolf as Archbishop of Olmütz; but it was not completed in time to be performed at the ceremony. It has at various times been sung, liturgically, in St Stephen's Cathedral, Vienna, and elsewhere, but it is too long and too subjective for liturgical use. It remains an extended and sublime meditation on the text of the Ordinary of the Mass which makes a Catholic—priest or layman—think anew about his faith.

We find here the first really profound musical expression of what the consecration means in the hushed reverence of the orchestral prelude after the *Sanctus* and—even if it is too prolonged—in the *Benedictus* that follows. The great work is too well known to need description in these pages, but, though no one would claim that Beethoven's ideas about religion were strictly orthodox, the *Missa Solemnis* must be regarded as a most inspiring charter of Catholic, and so of Christian, belief: and in the light of it, any attempts to de-Catholicize Beethoven can only end in being ridiculous.

Schubert's Masses are a different matter. The last two of them, A flat and E flat, have some fine music in the *Et incarnatus est* and *Sanctus* of the first, and above all in the moving and dramatic *Agnus Dei* of the second: but for the rest they are amiable and uneventful. Schubert is inexcusably careless about the text, not only missing out clauses in the *Credo* but uttering the strange dogma (in these Masses) *Confiteor unum baptisma in remissionem peccatorum mortuorum.*

Schubert, in fact, sat very lightly to his faith and spent his time among anti-clerical and free-thinking companions: but true religious feeling comes into a number of his songs, which are to be prized much more highly than his Masses.

CHERUBINI

Cherubini's following of the party line during the French Revolution, a matter of expediency, left his innate classicism undisturbed and the two Requiem Masses, in C minor and D minor, are the most liturgically minded sacred music that can be called great since the close of the sixteenth century. In general his Masses are free of the facile tunefulness and over-dramatization which is displayed in those by Leseur and Gossec, and are much superior to the often praised Masses by Hummel. Cherubini is guilty sometimes of sacrificing the text to the demands of symmetry and of over-elaboration but almost every one of his Masses contains imaginative vocal and orchestral writing. In the fine C minor Requiem Mass, which even Berlioz was constrained to admire, there is no straining after effect, there are no startling modulations. The words are mistress of the music. One must note the imaginative withholding of the violins until the *Dies irae,* the marvellous placing of the horn in the *Kyrie,* and above all the alternation of F minor and C major at the end of *Agnus Dei,* with what Cardinal Newman called "the lovely C which keeps recurring as the Requiem approaches eternity".

The D minor Requiem for three male voices and orchestra is even finer. Cherubini composed it, in his seventy-sixth year, for his own funeral. The tone of it is set by his use, at the start of the Introit, of the plainsong intonation. The unaccompanied Gradual far surpasses that of the C minor Mass and the compassionate setting of *Pie Jesu* is most moving. The one regrettable thing is the simultaneous singing of three different verses of *Dies irae*: a way of covering the ground quickly, but liturgically inadmissible. So, of course, strictly speaking, is the use of the orchestra in a Requiem Mass; but for that in these days permission may presumably be obtained.

It is interesting to note that in 1833, nine years before Cherubini's death, Dom Prosper Guéranger founded the Benedictine Congregation of France, best known as the Solesmes Benedictines, and began the great work of the reform of Gregorian chant which was to signalize the downfall of the Ratisbon edition of the chant, published by Frederich Pustet, who had obtained from Pius IX through the Sacred Congregation of Rites the sole right to publish the corrupt "Medicean" edition authorized by Paul V in 1614. The pope recognized the "Ratisbon" as the official edition of plainsong and imposed it on the whole Church. This was not, fortunately, an infallible pronouncement!

WITT, LISZT, BRUCKNER, GOUNOD, PEROSI

In 1867, Franz Xavier Witt (1834–88) founded the so-called "Cecilian" movement which was directed against the whole range of orchestral Masses. It called for a return to the Palestrina (*a capella*) style: and the result was a dreary and turgid stream of mainly completely unoriginal and imitative music.

Liszt was, to some extent, affected by this reactionary movement, though one would hardly think so in view of his declared intention, partly inspired by Princess Carolyn Wittgenstein, "to unite the means of the theatre and the church". (This had been well exploited ever since Monteverdi's *Vespers* and other church works of his Second Practice.)[4]

[4] See above, pp. 129–30.

Liszt's own smaller and simpler church works are worthy of revival; the Mass for four-part male choir and organ of 1848, or the *Missa Choralis* of 1865 (which makes considerable use of plainsong themes) or the Requiem for male voices of 1867–8. Liszt introduces into the latter some of the experimental harmonies of his later years: and these are even more prominent in his beautiful and moving *Via Crucis* of 1879, which is an oratorio. The chromaticism in these last works would have been strongly disapproved of by the Cecilians.

Of Bruckner's three fine Masses, D, E minor and F minor, the E minor, with accompaniment for woodwind and brass only, is an undoubted masterpiece and his festal *Te Deum*, disappointingly conventional in its closing pages, is also a splendid work. Very attractive, also, is Dvorak's *Te Deum*, a setting with enchanting touches in the orchestration that bring his beloved birds into the praise of God: but Verdi's *Te Deum* goes deeper than either of these. He asked that the manuscript should be placed under his pillow at his death and this touching request gives special emphasis to the last pages in which the solo soprano repeats *in te* (*Domine*) *speravi* three times, the appeal being punctuated by a high and shining trumpet-note before the chorus enter. Here, as in the Epilogue at the end of Berlioz's exquisite oratorio *L'Enfance du Christ,* his faith seems to revive.

No space need be wasted over Gounod's well-meant church music redolent with Catholicism *sucré,* but a word must be said about the fine work accomplished by Charles Bordes who, in 1897, founded, with Vincent D'Indy and Alexandre Guilmant, the *Schola Cantorum* for the performance and restoration of church music of the fifteenth and the seventeenth centuries and improvement in standard in modern church music.

There is a large number of religious works that were intended for concert hall rather than church, and so do not qualify as church music. Such are Rossini's, Dvorak's and

Verdi's settings of *Stabat Mater* (and, incidentally, Rossini's *Petite Messe Solennelle,* the very title of which, as it is a lengthy work, is a joke), Verdi's Requiem Mass and Dvorak's less fine and not to be despised work on the same theme.

The numerous Masses, motets and so forth of Lorenzo Perosi, who went in 1898 from the chapel of St Mark's, Venice, to be director of the Sistine Chapel, were over-praised in their time and are rarely now to be heard. César Franck's best church music is for the organ. Fauré's Requiem, not the work of a practising Catholic, is a simple and beautiful expression of trust in the mercy of God. He does not set the *Dies irae,* doubtless supposing the use of the plainsong. And so, at last, and with many omissions, we reach our own time.

CHAPTER IX

THE TWENTIETH CENTURY

In spite of economic difficulties and the ever increasing secularization of life many choirs, in churches large and small, continue to do good work today often with small encouragement in quarters where it should be forthcoming; and some splendid church music has been and is being composed that can stand comparison with the great achievements of the past. The 1914–18 War brought about a reaction against romanticism, causing composers to ignore the whole of the period associated with it and, with those of them who wrote church music, to study anew the sacred music of the centuries up to 1600. The results have been notable. We cannot say that liturgical music is in decline when we examine Kodály's *Missa Brevis,* Pizzetti's Requiem Mass, Stravinsky's, Rubbra's, Anthony Milner's and Lennox Berkeley's Masses, and the two fine Anglican contributions by Vaughan Williams, the Mass in G minor for double-choir, and Britten, *Missa Brevis* for boys' voices only, both composed for the Westminster Cathedral choir.

There is in these works no trace of operatic or oratorio style, of the use of stereotyped fugues, or of exaggerated emotionalism at the conventional points. Problems are faced freshly and solved so successfully that all these works can be called truly liturgical music. Kodály, for example, provides his Mass, which has organ accompaniment, with an instrumental *Introit* and *Ite missa est* as voluntaries to precede and follow each of these portions of the liturgy as opening and closing voluntaries, and he imaginatively sets the words *qui tollis peccata mundi* (which, of course, come in both *Gloria* and *Agnus Dei*) to the same shape of musical phrase. Pizzetti writes variations on the plainsong *Dies irae* in his setting of the sequence in his Requiem Mass for double-chorus with notable success: and only a purist would quarrel with the poignant vocalized "oh",[1] which at certain points so movingly accompanies the words of the Sequence. His *Agnus Dei* is most beautiful.

Vaughan Williams' Mass for soloists and double-choir is a splendidly forthright work with a mystical feeling in *Kyrie* and *Agnus Dei* which links him with Byrd, and a wonderful majesty of sound in *Gloria*, *Credo* and *Sanctus*.

Stravinsky, among contemporary composers, has been explicit about his views on church music. He holds that one must be a believer to compose it, "and not merely a believer in 'symbolic figures' but in the Person of the Lord, the person of the Devil and the miracles of the Church". "Music", he says, "is as well or better able to praise (God) than the building of the church and all its decoration: it is the Church's greatest ornament . . . religious music without religion is almost always vulgar."[2]

Stravinsky hoped that his Mass might be used liturgically but had no such aspiration for the *Threni*; "which is why I call it not *Tenebrae* but *Lamentations*".

There is no reason, except for its difficulty, why his Mass should not be used liturgically. It is scored for mixed chorus and double wood-wind quintet, and the average ear may have some difficulty at first in perceiving the union between the easily assimilated vocal parts and the harshly dissonant wood-

[1] One recalls Beethoven's poignant use of the ejaculation in the *Qui tollis* section of the *Gloria* in his *Missa solemnis*.

[2] These quotations are taken from *Conversations with Igor Stravinsky* by Igor Stravinsky and Robert Craft, pp. 123–4. Faber.

wind accompaniment. A wonderful effect is secured in the *Kyrie* by ending each petition on a consonance (in the modern sense) while the harmonic subtleties at *et homo factus est* and *crucifixus* are strokes of sheer genius. In *Agnus Dei*, anti-lyrical (as is the whole Mass), the words are unaccompanied throughout, the petitions being connected by short instrumental passages as uncompromising as those for the voices. The *dona nobis pacem* is another stroke of harmonic genius which puts the whole movement into proper perspective.

It is curious that while Stravinsky and Rubbra both allow for the priest's intonation in the *Credo* they give the first words of the *Gloria* to the choir—in Stravinsky's Mass to a solo voice. The intonation can, of course, be supplied.

Rubbra's four-part unaccompanied *Missa in honorem Sancti Dominici* is in length a *missa brevis* with *Credo*. In the latter the two upper voices poignantly sing *crucifixus* on one note three times while the lower two voices sing the whole clause to *sepultus est,* and at *Et in spiritum sanctum* the voices are divided into seven chordal parts up to *Et unum baptisma* with striking effect. *Sanctus, Benedictus* and *Agnus Dei* occupy no more than two pages of vocal score apiece in this remarkably concise and distinguished Mass.

Lennox Berkeley's four-part Mass, with an effectively written organ accompaniment, is more grateful vocally than Rubbra's and has a particularly beautiful *Sanctus*. The third in this trio of short Masses, by Benjamin Britten, is for boys' voices in three parts with organ accompaniment. It is full of the technical ingenuity and imaginative invention we associate with the composer. The texture is more unconventional than in Berkeley's Mass and may take a little getting used to, but the effort will be richly rewarded.

Mention must be made of Poulenc's series of motets for Holy Week which are superior musically to his rather contrived Mass: and of a number of motets, Mass and Office settings (Vespers and Compline) of a simplicity that brings them into the range of any choir of quite moderate accomplishment. Among these are Anthony Milner's congregational Vespers and Compline, Arthur Oldham's Mass for congregation, choir and organ, Lennox Berkeley's unison *Salve Regina* and Dorothy Howell's *Caeli enarrant* for two equal voices, all of which are typical of the good and valuable work being done in this field.

The time has fortunately gone by when music not good enough for theatre or concert hall went automatically into the Church, like the youngest sons of large Anglican middle-class families, but a large amount of splendid music of the great age of polyphony, or of the present time, goes unheard, while too much that is unworthy is still performed. There is no excuse for this, and it cannot be stated too often that the Encyclicals, *Motu proprio* and *Musicae Sacrae Disciplina*, like other papal pronouncements, have a juridical force. The latter Encyclical was declared by Mgr Romita, a consulter of the Sacred Congregation of the Council, to be "a solemn expression of the supreme *magisterium* given by Christ to his Vicar". Disobedience to it is an act of disloyalty to the Holy See.

In carrying out his task the Catholic composer is not limited to any one style of church music, provided the style chosen is consonant with liturgical ideals and purposes.

There is comfort in the thought that sincere musicians of all Christian Churches would not hesitate to subscribe to the noble words of the poet Robert Bridges, with which this chapter may fittingly end. It sums up the whole position.

Music being the universal expression of the mysterious and supernatural, the best that man has ever attained to, is capable of uniting in common devotion minds that are only separated by creeds, and it comforts our hope with a brighter promise of unity than any logic offers.

And if we consider and ask ourselves what sort of music we should wish to hear on entering a church, we should surely, in describing our ideal, say first of all that it must be something different from what is heard elsewhere; that it should be a sacred music, devoted to its purpose, a music whose peace should still passion, whose dignity should strengthen our faith, whose unquestioned beauty should find a home in our hearts, to cheer us in life and death; a music worthy of the fair temples in which we meet and of the holy words of our liturgy; a music whose expression of the mystery of things unseen never allowed any trifling motive to ruffle the sanctity of its reserve. What power for good such a music would have.[3]

[3] *Collected Essays*, XXI–XXVI, Oxford Univ. Press, p. 65.

CHAPTER X

THE LITURGICAL USE OF

THE ORGAN

This section will be confined to the use of the organ at liturgical functions, namely a high or sung Mass, Vespers and Compline. As its name indicates a set voluntary may or may not be played, as the organist decides, before the *Asperges me* (or *Vidi aquam*) at Mass, from the end of the Offertory to the start of the Preface, and at the end of Mass: or the organist may choose to improvise before and after Mass and be silent after the Offertory. At solemn Vespers the organist will be required to play during the incensation of the altar between the end of *Magnificat* and *Gloria Patri*.

It must be said at once that any other than brief improvisations should be left to musicians skilled in this difficult art: in less skilled hands it leads to mere "waffling", a series of sounds without musical shape or meaning. The line of great and less great organist-composers, which runs from Arnolt Schick (1460–after 1517) up to Bach, have provided the organist with a wealth of material, but the Catholic contribution, during this period, seems to be little known or used. This is all the more regrettable because a large amount of it is technically well within the range of the average organist, and a great deal of it is for manuals only. It needs certainly artistic taste, a study of the registrations appropriate to its time, with common-sense adaptation to the resources of the organs on which it will be played.[1]

Any organist of taste will wish to choose an entrance and middle voluntary (when a motet is not sung after the Offertory) that will be in accord with the spirit of the liturgy of the day and with the plainsong being used: and it so happens that the practice of writing organ "verses" for use at Vespers, which was prevalent from the sixteenth to the eighteenth centuries, and is still maintained in France, can be turned to good account. Historically this practice, deplorable liturgically, was intended to relieve the monotony of psalm singing, and it extended also to Mass. The organ alternated with the choir in sections brief enough, but naturally considerably longer than the plainsong. This use of the organ is not mentioned in the *Motu proprio, Musicae Sacrae Disciplina* or the Instruction of the Sacred Congregation of Rites, but the *Ceremoniale Episcoporum*, while tolerating it, directs that the missing text is to be recited audibly by choir and/or clergy: and that "it is commendable that a cantor should sing it to the organ accompaniment". This appears to be most impracticable advice.

The seven volumes in the series *Liber Organi*, edited by Ernst Kaller,[2] devoted to French, German, Italian and Spanish masters of the period named above, show what fine, if to modern ears somewhat austere, music the composition of "verses" called forth. In the two French volumes Jean Titelouze (1563–1633) sets four verses of the hymn *Veni Creator*, giving the plainsong melody, in long notes—each occupying one bar—to the pedals in all but the fourth verse, which is a *fugato*. In the third verse the two manual parts are in canon.

---

[1] Many modern organ builders have voiced their instruments so as to make "baroque registration" possible and many of the beautiful old instruments are in use.

[2] Published by Schott.

The same composer provides music for the third, sixth, eighth, tenth and twelfth (*Gloria Patri*) verses of *Magnificat*, with free writing, and François Couperin (1631–1703) writes "verses" for the various sections of the Mass.

In the Spanish volume we find verses by Antonio de Cabezon (1510–66) on the eight psalm tones which are each divided into four sections marked *choralis in cantu* (treble), *alto, tenore* and *basso* respectively. He treats the eight *Magnificat* tones in a very similar manner, but with six or seven sections to each tone.

There is a wealth of fine music in the *Fiori Musicali* published in 1635 (and diligently copied out by Bach) of the great Roman organist Girolamo Frescobaldi (1583–1643). It is said that 30,000 people flocked to his first recital at St Peter's, Rome, given when he was twenty-five years old. This must be a pious exaggeration.

The first piece in the book (Volume 5 of the Barenreiter edition) opens with a short "Toccata before Mass" and then has settings of the *Kyrie* of Mass XI (*Orbis factor*). There are twelve sections here, all but four being alternative versions. There is a fugal "Canzona after the Epistle" (forerunner of Mozart's *Epistle Sonatas*), a *Ricercar* (or study) after the *Credo*, the well-known chromatic "Toccata for the Elevation" and a "*Canzona* after the Communion". Similar movements follow including two other Toccatas for the Elevation, one of great length. The liturgy does not now allow of any of these pieces in the Mass being used as intended, but the organist can make excellent use of them as voluntaries.

The volume *Classici Italiani dell' Organo,* edited by Ireneo Faser (Zanzibon, Padua) contains a splendid selection of similar material, including compositions by Girolamo Cavazzoni (*c.* 1480) (more fully represented in the series *I Classici della musica Italiana* edited by Gabrielle d'Annunzio and now hard to obtain) based—as is nearly all his work

—on plainsong themes,[3] by Andrea and Giovanni Gabrielli, Claudio Merulo (1533–1604) and Annibale Padovano, Michelangelo Rossi (1598–1653), Bernardo Pasquini (1637–1710) and Domenico Zipoli. This last composer (1688–1776) was organist at the church of Jesus in Cordoba (Argentina): his music is exceptionally fresh and melodious, and his *Pastorale*, one of his best-known pieces, could suitably be played at Christmas. Another valuable collection is *Les Maîtres français de l'Orgue* (seventeenth and eighteenth centuries), fifty pieces edited by Felix Rangel, and one of the many fine editions published by the *Schola Cantorum*.

There are exquisite pieces here by such composers as Nicolas le Begue, Nicolas de Grigny and Guillaume de Nivers. One of the most attractive is the *Noël sur les flûtes* by Louis-Claude d'Aquin. Most of these pieces are for one manual without pedals.

The Mulliner Book (Volume 1 of *Musica Britannica*) edited by Denis Stevens, contains, among some secular material, many admirable pieces by the Elizabethan composers Blitheman, Johnson, Shepherd and Tallis based on plainsong melodies, a selection of which are published by Stainer and Bell; Barenreiter publishes some church pieces, from various sources, edited by Professor Stevens, under the title *Altenglische Orgelmusik* (for manuals only).

The outgoing voluntary leaves a greater freedom of choice to the organist. A Bach chorale-prelude would be inappropriate as an ingoing or middle voluntary as being based on melodies not in accord with plainsong, but could well be used after Mass, as could a prelude and fugue by any of the German Lutheran masters, or one of the sets by Brahms, Reger or Karg-Elert. There is place here, also, for some of the works of the brilliant school of French organist composers

[5] The latter volume contains a section for the complete ordinaries of three plainsong Masses, including *Orbis factor* (XI) and twelve Office hymns, one section to each of them.

of the nineteenth century, Lemmens, Guilmant, Widor and Franck; but care must be taken in selection of their works. For the concluding voluntary, in fact, there is an enormous choice open. Anglican composers also offer much good work here.

The French school, however, have the most to offer the Catholic organist. In the series *La Schola Paroissiale* there are excellent works by Déodat de Sévérac, Louis Vierne's *Messe Basse* and his *24 pièces en Style Libre* (Durand). Very valuable also are Guilmant's *60 Interludes dans la Tonalité Grégorienne* (Schott) and Gigout's *Cent Pièces Brèves dans la tonalité de plainchant* (Heugel) and *Album Grégorien* (2 volumes, Léduc). Charles Tournemire composed a vast work, *L'Orgue mystique* (Heugel) containing 255 pieces for the liturgical year. These pieces are uneven in value but many are of excellent quality.

Finally Oliver Messiaen, the most distinguished of French composers and, from a conservative point of view, the most controversial. Only very accomplished organists could hope to play his difficult music but when it is played with the requisite technique and imagination it makes a profound impression. One of his most accessible and beautiful works is *La Nativité du Seigneur,* nine meditations on the birth of our Lord. Messiaen, much attracted in later years to Indian music and bird-song, is, at heart, a profoundly Catholic composer.

From what has been said above there is a wide field open to the Catholic organist and one which needs to be explored much more fully than it has been.

CHAPTER XI

DE SACRA MUSICA ET SACRA LITURGIA

The *Instruction* of the Sacred Congregation of Rites, promulgated on September 3rd, 1958, the feast of St Pius X, is a lengthy and comprehensive document of 118 sections, of which some 65 are devoted to music. Canon J. B. O'Connell, who has translated the Latin text into English and provided an excellent commentary (*Sacred Music and Liturgy*, 1959), points out that "the musical parts are not technical but treat of the liturgical aspects of music, and the rubrics that govern it". One may, perhaps, be permitted to regret, with all due respect, that in one or two of the sections the findings of modern musicology have not been taken into account. Thus "sacred polyphony" is vaguely defined as "that kind of music composed for a number of voices in measured rhythm, *derived from Gregorian melodies, and without instrumental accompaniment* which began to flourish in the *Latin Church in medieval times*" (italics, the author's). The *Motu proprio* of Pius X had declared that "the classic polyphony of the Roman School had reached its greatest perfection in the sixteenth century, owing to the works of Pierluigi da Palestrina". It has been made abundantly clear in this book that composers of sacred polyphony used material from pre-existent sources other than Gregorian melodies and it was also said that *a*

capella or unaccompanied polyphony was specially associated
with the papal chapel, instruments being in frequent use elsewhere. This section of the *Instruction* gives the wrong impression historically. The use of instrumental accompaniment in
"Modern Sacred Music" is allowed for in (7), and in (8)
direction is given as to what kind of organ music is allowable.
It must comply exactly with the laws of sacred music. This
important ruling has been mentioned in the chapter on organ
music in the present book.

The *Instruction,* in (10), makes a clear distinction between
sacred and religious music. It is allowed that the latter, if
"from the intention of the composer and from its content and
purpose (it) strives to express pious and religious sentiments",
will be "a powerful aid to religion": but "as it is not intended for divine worship and displays a rather free character
it is not allowed in liturgical functions".

All oratorios or semi-dramatic musical compositions on a
sacred theme, performed by soloists, chorus and orchestra,
are therefore excluded. This section obviously refers to such
works as the Requiem Masses of Verdi, Dvorak, Berlioz,
Fauré, settings of *Stabat Mater* by Verdi, Dvorak, Szyma-
nowski, Poulenc, Lennox Berkeley, etc. In (20) permission is
given for such works to be performed "at exercises of piety",
and (55) lays down that their proper place is "the concert
hall, or a hall set aside for entertainments or meetings, not
the church, sacred to the worship of God". The local Ordinary,
however, may allow such a concert in a church (or oratory
of any kind).

The *Instruction* idealistically visualizes, in (24), the congregation taking part not only in the Ordinary but also in the
Proper of the Mass, if sufficiently skilled, but is realistic in
requiring the faithful at least to learn the easier plainsong
Masses, recommending a conflation of Masses XV, XVI,
Credos I or III (in the *Kyriale*). It is interesting that in (27)
more than one verse of the Introit psalm may be sung if

required and that after the Offertory antiphon the disused verses of the Offertory may be sung. These verses are to be found in a volume edited by Carolus Ott (*Offertoriale sive Versus Offertoriorum,* Desclée).

In the same section a "sacred silence", except when *Benedictus* has to be sung, should be encouraged up to *Pater Noster*. This should eliminate indeterminate drooling on the organ. A Latin motet after the Communion, antiphon or verses of the psalm from which it is taken, can be sung if the distribution of Holy Communion is prolonged. Eucharistic Benediction is recognized in (47) as "a true liturgical function", and the studies of musicologists are encouraged in (49). In (59) the *Instruction* refers briefly to the rhythmic problem in Gregorian chant, permitting the rhythmical signs of Solesmes (not so named) but in any such undertaking demanding that "the value and nature of the notes, as now found in the Vatican books of liturgical chant, be respected in their entirety". There was reason for caution here, especially as approval had once been given to the corrupt Ratisbon edition of the chant.

In (60) the use of musical instruments is considered and those "so associated with profane music that they are entirely unfit for sacred use", are disallowed. Which are these? One recalls Ps. 55. However, Pius X had allowed "a limited section carefully made of wind instruments", so that Bruckner's E minor Mass and Stravinsky's Mass are presumably within the law. It is a pity that, in (70), the drums, together with bells and cymbals, are designated as "noisy or frivolous". They need not be either.

Finally one may, again with respect, regret that "organists, choir masters, singers, musicians and others attached to the service of the Church" should be expected to "give their services gratuitously in the interest of piety and religion and for the love of God, and they should be encouraged to do so", inasmuch that the clergy may feel encouraged, for their part, to pay musicians less than they do at present—which is little enough. Provision is made, however, for a "just salary" to those unable to give their services gratis—that is to professional musicians. If in a church of any size the music is to be directed, as it should be, by a skilled musician, his services should be properly rewarded.

The care for sacred music and the liturgy embodied in the *Instruction* reflects the high ideals given expression to at various times in the long history of the Church, and many centres of liturgical activity, whether in the smallest village church or the grandest cathedral, are spreading these ideals far and wide. They need and deserve our constant prayers that the ears and eyes of men may be opened wide to the wonderful spiritual and artistic richness of the Catholic heritage in both these closely related fields. Several sections of the *Instruction* deal with the difficult subject of "popular religious chant" which may be freely used in exercises of piety but is strictly governed when used in liturgical functions (13–15–19). There are many excellent hymns in the vernacular but also many that are banal in both words and music though well loved by the people. This also is true of repository art. Mass-produced statues and pictures can awaken piety as can trivial hymns. There is no easy answer to these facts; the only solution seems to lie in the gradual elimination of base material and the further education of the faithful.[1]

[1] The revised *Westminster Hymnal* (1940) and the *St Basil Hymnal* (1958) are an improvement on their predecessors, but the excellent new material seems to make little headway with conservative congregations who want the "old tunes". The subject is well treated in the relevant chapter of *The Music of Catholic Hymnody* by Erik Routley (Independent Press, 1957).

SELECT BIBLIOGRAPHY

In this series: AMIOT, F.: *History of the Mass*; DALMAIS, I.-H.: *The Eastern Liturgies*; SPEAIGHT, Robert: *The Christian Theatre*.

The New Oxford History of Music: Volume I, edited by Egon Wellesz, *Ancient and Oriental Music*; Volume II, edited by Dom Anselm Hughes, *Early Medieval Music up to 1300*; Volume III, edited by Gerald Abraham, *Ars Nova and the Renaissance*: London and New York, Oxford Univ. Press, 1957, 1954, 1960.

APEL, Willi: *Gregorian Chant*, London, Burns & Oates, 1958, and Bloomington, Ind., Indiana Univ. Press, 1957; *Harvard Dictionary of Music*, Cambridge, Mass, Harvard Univ. Press, 1944, and London, Foyles, 1945.

APEL, Willi, and DAVISON, A. T.: *Historical Anthology of Music:* Volume I, *Oriental, Medieval and Renaissance Music;* Volume II, *Baroque, Rococo and Pre-Classical Music*, London and New York, Oxford Univ. Press, 1947 and 1950.

BRIDGES, Robert: *Collected Essays*, London and New York, Oxford Univ. Press, 1935.

BUKOFZER, Manfred: *Studies in Medieval and Renaissance Music*, London, Dent, 1952, and New York, Norton, 1950.

HARRISON, Frank: *Music in Medieval Britain*, London, Kegan Paul, 1958.

JUNGMANN, J. A., S.J.: *The Mass of the Roman Rite, Its Origins Development* (Missarum Solemnia), translated by F. A. Brunner, C.SS.R., two volumes, New York, Benziger, 1951 and 1955, and London, Burns & Oates, 1957.

LANG, Paul: *Music in Western Civilisation*, London, Dent, 1942. *New St Basil's Hymnal*, Cincinatti, Ohio, Willis Music, 1958.

OTT, C.: *Offertoriale, sive versus Offertoriorum*, Tournai, Desclée, 1935.

REESE, Gustave: *Music in the Middle Ages*, London, Dent, 1941, and New York, Norton, 1940; *Music in the Renaissance*, London, Dent, and New York, Norton, 1954.

ROBERTSON, Alec, and STEVENS, Denis: *The Pelican History of Music*, volume I, *Ancient Forms to Polyphony*, Harmondsworth and Baltimore, Penguin, 1960 (the first of three volumes planned).

STEVENS, Denis: *Tudor Church Music*, London, Faber, 1961.

STRAVINSKY, Igor, and CRAFT, Robert: *Conversations with Igor Stravinsky*, London, Faber, 1959.

VOLLAERTS, G.: *Rhythmic Proportions in Early Medieval Ecclesiastical Chant*, Leiden, Brill, 1958.

WAGNER, Peter: *Introduction to the Gregorian Melodies*, London, Plainsong and Medieval Music Society, 1901.

WERNER, Eric: *The Sacred Bridge*, London, Dobson, 1959.

The Twentieth Century Encyclopedia
of Catholicism

*The number of each volume indicates its place in
the over-all series and not the order of publication.*

TWENTIETH CENTURY ENCYCLOPEDIA OF CATHOLICISM

All titles are subject to change.